D0441628

Cycling the U.S. Parks

50 Scenic Tours in America's National Parks

Jim Clark

Bicycle Books – San Francisco

Copyright © 1991 Jim Clark

First printing 1993

Printed in the U.S.A.

Cover design: Kent Lytle
Cover photograph: Neil van der Plas

Frontispiece photo: Yosemite National Park, California

All photographs by the author

Maps by Meridian Mapping, Oakland

Published by:
Bicycle Books, Inc.
PO Box 2038
Mill Valley, CA 94492
U.S.A.

Distributed to the book trade by:
USA: National Book Network, Lanham, MD
Canada: Raincoast Book Distribution, Vancouver, BC
UK: Chris Lloyd Sales and Marketing, Poole, Dorset

Publisher's Cataloging in Publication Data:
Jim Clark, 1959—
Cycling the U.S. Parks: 50 Scenic Tours in America's National
Parks. Series title: The Active Travel Series
Bibliography: p. Includes Index.
1. Bicycles and Cycling—touring guides.
2. National parks, recreational use.
I. Title
II. Authorship

Library of Congress Catalog Card No. 92-83825

ISBN 0-933201-56-7, Paperback original

Dedication

I want to dedicate this book to my wife, Vicki. For it was her deep understanding and incredible unselfishness that enabled me to take the time necessary during the summer of 1989 to travel to each of the national parks where I personally cycled all of the routes discussed in this book.

It was this same understanding during the years which followed that allowed me to focus on writing the manuscript, when often it would have been easier to do other things.

Thank you too for all of those hours you spent typing those seemingly endless revisions.

I want to also thank Marie for her help caring for our three year old son Michael while Vicki and I spent time working on the manuscript.

About the Author

Jim Clark is a certified public accountant, who during his 10- year career has held management positions with several companies ranging in sales from 10 to 250 million. He is also a self- employed income tax preparer.

Jim got his first bike at age 10 and by age 12 had taken several trips of a hundred miles or more in a single day to destinations in Illinois and Wisconsin.

At age 13, he mapped out an 80 day 8,000 mile bicycle journey around the United States that he planned to take the summer after he would graduate from high school. That trip never materialized due to a job, as well as college planning and registration.

Shortly after beginning college Jim updated his trip plans, expanding it to 12,000 miles and covering a majority of this country's major national parks. But upon graduation from DePaul University in 1982, he obtained employment as an accountant and again put his dream on hold.

Finally, in 1989, after gaining a number of years experience in the business world and upon reaching age 30, Jim again made plans for a bicycle trip through the national parks. It must have been the effect of reaching that magic age of 30 and the tremendous support of his wife Vicki hat made the difference. This time, the long awaited journey was made.

During the summer of 1989, Jim personally cycled each one of the tours recommended in this book. Jim, Vicki, and their three year old son Michael live in Crystal Lake, Illinois.

TABLE OF CONTENTS

Introduction

This is a book about adventure, relaxation, and enjoyment of the great outdoors. It is a book that combines two of my great loves: cycling and the national parks. This book will explore thirty of our national parks, from the coast of Maine to southwest Texas to the Olympic Peninsula of Washington. Fifty bicycle routes, ranging from a 4-mile jaunt at Cape Cod National Seashore to a 96-mile journey along the Lower Loop of Yellowstone National Park, will be described, highlighting the key points of interest along each route while also giving you an idea of the land and terrain through which each route passes.

The National Park Idea

The national park idea grew out of the farsightedness of men like John Muir, Theodore Roosevelt, Cornelius Hedges, and Frederick Law Olmsted, who each in their own way laid the groundwork for today's national park system.

Frederick Law Olmsted, the well-traveled, wilderness-loving landscape architect who designed Central Park in New

Many of the National Parks are in the West. Olympic National Park in Washington.

York City, provided the impetus for the first step toward a national park system. After a pleasure trip to Yosemite Valley more than a century ago, he and a group of associates persuaded Congress to pass a bill, which President Lincoln signed in 1864, preserving Yosemite Valley "for public use, resort and recreation."

Cornelius Hedges, a Montana attorney, was a member of a famous exploring party known as the Washburn-Langford-Doane expedition that in 1870 surveyed the wonders of Yellowstone. On their last night before returning home after a month of exploration, the group held a campfire meeting. Little did they know that this meeting, held along the confluence of the Madison, Gibbons, and Firehole rivers in western Yellowstone, would become historic. Under the laws of the day, all were entitled to stake claims on the land and its natural marvels. As the men were discussing how they would divide this wonderland among themselves, Hedges made a far-reaching proposal. He proposed that they work for the preservation of the whole area under government protection. The men enthusiastically endorsed the idea, and after their return, several of them campaigned for a law to set aside the area. Their presentation was so effective that Congress passed the necessary legislation only seventeen months after their return, thus creating Yellowstone as this country's first national park.

Some, however, were more interested in areas like Yosemite Valley and Yellowstone for their own benefit rather than the benefit of the people. Lumbermen and ranchers were a constant threat to Yosemite Valley. A Scot by the name of John Muir became the valley's champion. Muir was a passionate and articulate spokesman for conservation before either the term or the idea were fashionable, and his pleas for the wilderness led to the establishment of a "forest reservation" of a million acres in Yosemite Valley.

But it was not until 1903, when Muir and President Theodore Roosevelt camped together in the valley, and Roosevelt became enthralled both with the scenery and with Muir's point of view, that the conservation movement found an ally powerful enough to ensure its survival.

The Advantages of Cycling in the Parks

Cycling is an outstanding way to enjoy the parks. Unlike a car, bus, or other vehicle, on a bike you are able to experience the smells, sounds, and spectacular scenery from an unimpaired vantage point. The pace is much slower on a bike, allowing you to expand the dimensions of time to more fully enjoy the many aspects of the parks you might have missed from a car. So whether it's cycling through the evergreen-scented forests of Acadia, the Grand Tetons, Lassen, or Glacier; or biking along the national seashores of Cape Cod, Cape Hatteras, Padre Island, or Point Reyes, where the sounds of ocean surf and feeding sea birds prevail, the memories of your ride through a national park will stay with you for a lifetime.

The freedom and flexibility of cycling in the national parks is beyond comparison. You are able to stop literally anywhere without getting in someone's way, enabling you to get that once-in-a-lifetime photo of wildlife or scenes that you might have missed from a car because vehicles normally can only stop at turnouts and not on the road. Also, on a bike you are able to approach animals that you normally would not see along the road in a car, as the noise from the approaching car would have long before scared them away.

Cycling through the parks also allows you to breeze into— or for that matter completely avoid—congested turnouts and overlooks where drivers struggle to find parking spaces.

Finally, there is the feeling of being one with nature. In addition to the sights, sounds, and smells you experience, the satisfaction you achieve in cycling the incredible ascents to such places as Trail Ridge Road, Going-to-the-Sun-Highway, Hurricane Ridge, and the Tioga Road—as well as the joy of coasting back down these magnificent roads—is quite a thrill.

About this Book

The book is organized into six geographic regions of the country. Each region has a short introduction that briefly familiarizes you with each park in that region as well as the special attractions you can visit along each of the bicycle routes. Each chapter covers a separate park and is formatted in the following way. The narrative will first introduce you to the park's history, geology, and special points of interest to be explored, before giving a detailed guide and account of the bicycle routes taken through each park. Toward the end of

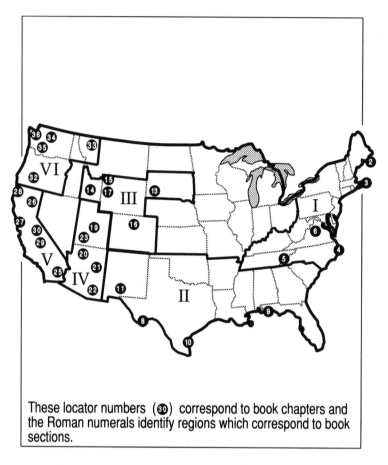

These locator numbers (30) correspond to book chapters and the Roman numerals identify regions which correspond to book sections.

each chapter, there is a summary of additional popular activities to enjoy at each of the parks as well as a practical guide. The guide gives the distance of each bicycle route, type of terrain to be encountered, details regarding access to the parks, and accommodations to be found in and around each of the national parks.

1. Introduction to the Eastern Parks

The parks of the East include Acadia National Park in Maine, Cape Cod National Seashore in Massachusetts, Cape Hatteras National Seashore in North Carolina, Great Smoky Mountains National Park along the border of North Carolina and Tennessee, and Shenandoah National Park in Virginia.

Acadia is a land much influenced by the glaciers of the last ice age. From its coastline to its valleys to its highlands, all show signs or are the result of the mile-thick rivers of ice that once covered the entire region. The bicycle rides at Acadia take you through fern-filled forests and along surf-sprayed coastline, passing such attractions as Cadillac Mountain, the highest point on the East Coast shoreline at 1,530 feet; Thunder Hole, an ocean-carved chasm that slaps back the Atlantic tides with a loud boom; and Otter Point, where birdwatching is quite popular. Inland, 43 miles of carriage paths offer many different routes for cyclists to choose from. Some of these carriage paths cross hand-cut granite stone bridges, sixteen of

Golden grasslands stretch out across Cades Cove as morning clouds and fog drift by the distant mountains in the Great Smokies National Park.

which were built along the paths between the years 1917 and 1933.

Cape Cod is a wonderful park to cycle in. Several trails take you through forest, along marsh and, of course, sand dunes. The dunes appear stationary, but they are undergoing constant change. Cape Cod is rich in history, too, for this is where the pilgrims first landed in 1620. Each bicycle trail has its own special features. For instance, the Cape Cod Rail Trail leads you through forest while offering many beautiful views of Cape Cod Bay. The Nauset Trail passes marshland on its way to the surf of the Atlantic. The Head of the Meadow Trail passes Pilgrim Spring for a touch of history. And the Province Lands Trail takes you among the park's most impressive sand dunes and on to Race Point where whales are often seen off the coast.

Cape Hatteras National Seashore is located on the Outer Banks of North Carolina. These are barrier islands that have long protected the mainland from the direct onslaught of tropical hurricanes. The bicycle routes take you to the Cape Hatteras Lighthouse, tallest in the U.S. at 208 feet, the coastline near Diamond Shoals, and through the Pea Island Wildlife Refuge. Other attractions at Cape Hatteras include Fort Raleigh, where the Lost Colony vanished in 1586, and the Wright Brothers National Memorial just south of Kill Devil Hills, where the first airplane flight occurred in 1903.

The Great Smoky Mountains exist today much as they did hundreds of years ago. The fertile soils and abundant rain encourage a remarkable diversity of plant life. In fact, the area is world-renowned for its variety of flora, and nowhere else of similar size in North America is there such plant diversity. The bicycle rides in the Great Smokies take you through Cades Cove, a place that cyclists absolutely fall in love with. Its rolling hills and sprawling golden meadows are encircled by the ever-changing colors of the forested mountainsides of the Smokies. On your ride through the cove you can visit restored log cabins and a cable mill, and learn the history of the people who farmed this land. You can also visit the Clingman's Dome, where an observation tower enables spectacular views of the park. The Appalachian Trail winds through the park, and the Blue Ridge Parkway begins near the Oconaluftee Visitor Center.

Shenandoah National Park lies astride a beautiful section of the Blue Ridge. Providing vistas of the spectacular landscape is Skyline Drive, a winding road that runs along the Blue

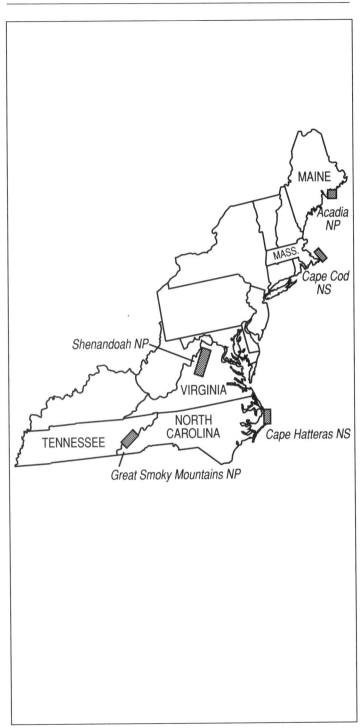

Ridge through the length of the park. The park's main attractions are really the countless scenic views the many overlooks provide of the Shenandoah Valley to the west and the rolling hills and ridges of the Piedmont country to the east. During the autumn, many visitors are drawn to the park to view the magnificent fall colors that set the forested hillsides ablaze in a kaleidoscope of changing colors.

LEGEND

❶	BIKE RIDES	⊓	PICNIC AREA
▲	CAMPING SITE	■	POINT OF INTEREST
⤝	CAVE, TUNNEL	🕴	RESTROOMS
○	CITY/TOWN	⌢	RIVER, CREEK
👥	INFORMATION	—	ROADS
⊗	LAKE	—	ROUTE
ⵎ	LIGHTHOUSE	●	START OR END OF ROUTE
→	ONE WAY TRAVEL	⋯	TRAIL
⁓	PARK BOUNDARY	═	WATERFALL
▲	PEAK	🏨	YOUTH HOSTEL

In some instances, because of space limitations, point symbols are not in their exact location – placement of the symbol is meant to indicate general vicinity.

2. Maine: Acadia National Park

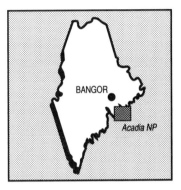

On the New England coast in the state of Maine, about fifty miles southeast of Bangor, lies Acadia National Park. It is a place of rugged surf-sprayed coastline, glacier-carved granite peaks and quiet fern-filled forests of pine, fir, and spruce.

Most of Acadia sits atop Mount Desert Island, which in large part was shaped by the most recent ice age. Its highest point, Cadillac Mountain at 1,530 feet, is also the highest point anywhere on the East Coast shoreline. Observing this peak as well as neighboring peaks it becomes apparent how massive glaciers over a mile thick scoured down the smooth, rounded highlands seen today.

Not so apparent are the valleys scooped out by glacial ice that now form Eagle Lake and Jordan Pond, Echo Lake and Long Pond. Located between these lakes and ponds is the

Eagle Lake in Acadia National Park, Maine.

deepest fjord on the eastern coast of the United States, Somes Sound. A fjord is the seaward segment of a valley cut by the glacial ice and later submerged by the sea. It is about six miles long and plunges between rocky banks to a depth of 150 feet.

Blanketing these mountains and skirting the shores of these ponds and lakes are the forests of Acadia. Many varieties of coniferous and deciduous trees can be found here, and ferns are abundant. It is through this forest that the carriage paths wind.

Between sea and land is the tidal zone. Specially adapted organisms live in tidepools created and in constant flux due to the effect of Acadia's tides, which occur twice daily and range from 9 to 14 feet.

Acadia was discovered by French explorer Samuel De Champlain when he sailed into the bay in 1604. During the French and Indian War between France and England, French frigates hid from English men-of-war in Frenchman Bay, screened from detection by the Porcupine Islands.

Acadia's more recent history is unusual because the park was neither carved out of public lands nor bought with public funds. It was envisioned and donated through the efforts of private citizens. Maine residents and summer visitors alike donated their time and resources to preserve Acadia's beauty. George B. Dorr and Charles W. Eliot, a former president of Harvard University, saw the dangers of development and acted to avoid them. John D. Rockefeller, Jr., built the carriage paths and gave more than eleven thousand acres, about one-third of the park's area, to what became known as Acadia National Park.

The bicycle rides in Acadia National Park include a shorter 10-mile jaunt around Eagle Lake and a 30-mile ramble along Park Loop Road. The Eagle Lake route is excellent for family rides.

Begin the Eagle Lake ride from the Hulls Cove Visitor Center by taking a narrow footpath from the southern end of the visitor center parking lot through thick forest for about half a mile to the carriage path that will take you to Witch Hole Pond.

Rapidly, you are enveloped by the forests of Acadia. The trees are not tall, but the forest of pine, birch, and other hardwoods is thick. The more common sounds of civiliza-tion are left behind as the sounds of nature become more prevalent. When you reach the carriage path, head toward Witch Hole Pond. At the pond take a left for spectacular views of Frenchman Bay and the Porcupine Islands. Brightly colored lobster buoys can be seen in the bay. Each lobsterman has his own set of colors that are registered with the state.

The trail continues to wind through forest on your way to Eagle Lake. Along the northern end of Eagle Lake, the land to the left of the carriage path slopes upward on its way to Cadillac Mountain, while the peaceful waters of the lake are immediately to the right. The 5-mile path around the lake offers many beautiful views across the water and the hills beyond. Upon completion of this loop around Eagle Lake, rejoin the trail to Witch Hole Pond that will take you back to Hulls Cove Visitor Center. The round-trip distance is about ten miles and will take 2 to 3 hours to complete at a leisurely pace.

Like the Eagle Lake ride, begin the Park Loop Road route from the visitor center. This road, unlike the gravel carriage paths, is an asphalt-surfaced road that is open to motor vehicles; however, the speed limits are slow. Also, 12 of the approximate 30 miles are on a one-way road.

Shortly after leaving the visitor center, you will come to a beautiful view of Frenchman Bay, Schoodic Peninsula, Bar Harbor, and the open Atlantic to the east. Just up the road from here is an area of about ten thousand acres that was burned during a month-long fire in 1947.

Several miles farther along the route, you arrive at an overlook with a view of Sand Beach far below. The Shore Path

The Maine coastline just north of Otter Point.

Trailhead leads sunbathers and swimmers brave enough to challenge the 55-degree water to the beach.

Continuing on, you are in constant view of the Atlantic surf as it roars against the rocky shoreline. You can see and hear gulls and cormorants as they feed along the coast. Fir and spruce trees line the winding route. Occasionally you can see a windjammer out at sea. Soon, you come to Thunder Hole, where an ocean-carved chasm slaps back the tidal rush with a loud boom. Many tourists stop here.

Moving on, you soon reach Otter Point, where a trail can take you through thick spruce and on to steep cliffs and ledges, an area frequented by many feeding seabirds. Your route turns briefly inland as you negotiate in and around a very serene Otter Cove, before returning to the rugged rocky coastline for another mile or so.

Eagle Lake

Distance: 10 miles, nice family trail.

Terrain: Generally level, a few small hills.

Park Loop Road

Distance: 30 miles

Terrain: Generally level, several gradual grades.

Bicycle Rental: Available in Bar Harbor and other nearby towns.

Accommodations: Tourist services are available in Bar Harbor and surrounding villages. The park also has two campgrounds, Blackwoods where reservations are required and Seawall which is first-come, first-served. Bear Brook and Fabbri picnic areas are located along the park loop road. Pickup park handout on suggested bike trails located throughout the park.

Access: Take I-95 to US 1 for a scenic ride along Maine's coastline to Maine 3 to the park if you are approaching from the south. From the west or north, take US 2 or I-95 to Alt. 1 near Bangor to Maine 3 to the park. The closest major airports are located in Bangor, Augusta, or Portland.

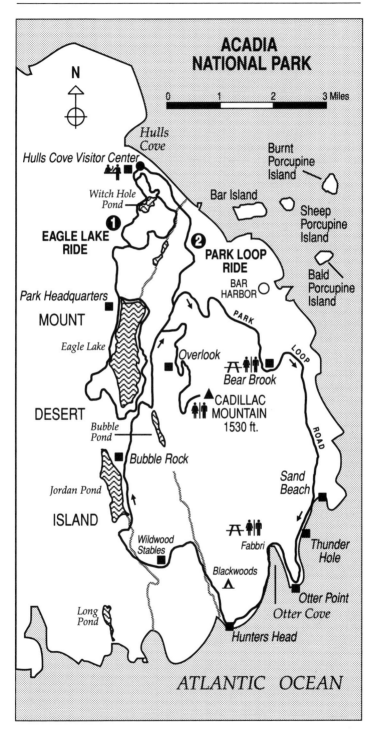

At Hunters Head the route turns inland once again, away from the salty air of the coastline and into the smell of pine as you enter the forest near Wildwood Stables. You next come to Jordan Pond, one of the many ponds and lakes cut by the mighty glaciers of the last ice age. Bubble Rock still lies rather precariously on a high cliff just where a retreating glacier left it eons ago.

Approaching Eagle Lake, the route is slightly elevated, allowing picturesque views across the shimmering waters lit up by the late afternoon sun. From this point, the last 5 miles to the visitor center are an enjoyable downhill. Just before passing Eagle Lake, a road to the right leads to the top of Cadillac Mountain. It is a steep 8% grade, but the views from the top are worth the effort.

Soon you are back at the Hulls Cove Visitor Center. The afternoon ride is over, but the memories of crashing surf, feeding gulls, and pine-scented forest will linger in your mind.

Other activities include hiking. Foot trails are plentiful and range from easy lowland paths to rugged mountain routes. Horseback riding is popular along the carriage paths that are open to horses. Rent them at the Wildwood Stables along Park Loop Road. Naturalist programs include boat cruises, and seashore, woodland, and mountaintop walks.

For water lovers, swimming is popular at Sand and Echo beaches. Fishing in fresh and saltwater is permitted. Windjammers provide fascinating side excursions to some of the small islands that cars cannot reach.

For snowbunnies, there is cross-country skiing and snowshoeing; snowmobiling is allowed along the carriage paths. Ice fishing and winter hiking are also popular. Winter season at Acadia National Park lasts from November to April, depending on snowfall.

3. Massachusetts: Cape Cod National Seashore

Cape Cod National Seashore is located about a hundred miles southeast of Boston on a narrow strip of land that boldly pushes out into the Atlantic only to be bent back by the power of the ocean waves. In fact, this strip of land, scarcely more than five miles wide in most places, is what geologists call a moraine. A moraine is a ridge of debris such as stones, sand, and earth left by a retreating glacier from the last ice age.

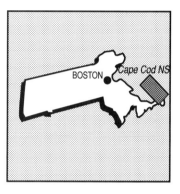

Cape Cod is a land of sand dunes. The most spectacular dunes are at the cape's tip in an area north of Pilgrim Heights and on west to Race Point and Herring Cove Beach. Although appearing stationary to the naked eye, the dunes are constantly changing, especially during storms when great waves and

Near Race Point, the Province Lands Trail cuts through a section of dunes where grasses, bushes and trees have established a firm foothold in the sandy soil.

gale-force winds relentlessly pound at their surface. Vegetation becomes very important in this regard, for where grasses can anchor themselves in the dunes the process can be slowed. As the dune movement slows and the grasses thicken, various bushes and trees can begin to grow, further anchoring the

Nauset Trail

Distance: 5 miles, nice family trail

Terrain: Generally level

Cape Cod Rail Trail

Distance: 30 miles, nice family trail

Terrain: Level

Head of the Meadow Trail

Distance: 4 miles, nice family trail

Terrain: Level

Province Lands Trail

Distance: 8 miles, nice family trail

Terrain: Hilly, many small hills

Bicycle Rental: Available within the towns of Cape Cod.

Accommodations: Tourist services are available in Chatham, Orleans, Eastham, Wellfleet, Truro, and Provincetown near the cape's tip. The park service does not operate a campground, but Nickerson State Park in nearby Brewster offers camping on a first-come, first-served basis. Picnic areas and restrooms are located along each of the four suggested bike routes covered in this chapter. Pickup park handout on bike trails.

Access: From Providence, take I-195 to Massachusetts 25 to US 6 to the seashore. From Boston, take Massachusetts 3 to US 6 to the seashore. Flights operate between Hyannis and Boston, Providence and New York, and also between Boston and Provincetown.

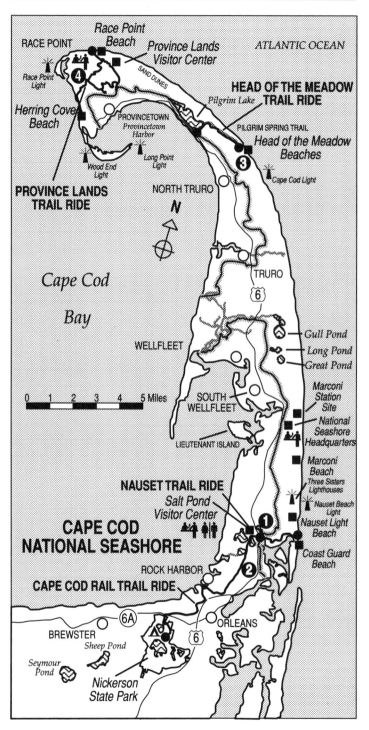

dune. By observing several of the pictures in this chapter you can see how the process occurs.

Cape Cod has a human history that is rich indeed. It was in the Provincetown area that the Pilgrims landed in 1620 before sailing across the bay to Plymouth. Near Pilgrim Heights on the Head of the Meadow Trail is Pilgrim Spring, where it is believed the Pilgrims obtained their first fresh water in the new world.

After Plymouth was established, Cape Cod was soon settled by fishermen and whalers. As a matter of fact, the Great Island, which is now connected to the mainland, is where whalers used to congregate. Whales can be seen even today from the seashore, especially near Race Point.

Cape Cod National Seashore has several bike trails to choose from. Each gives a distinct look at the seashore's environment. The trails are short and excellent for leisurely family rides.

The Nauset Trail originates from the Salt Pond Visitor Center and ends at Coast Guard Beach. Leaving the visitor center, you head east into a thick but low forest. The soil on Cape Cod is poor for plant development, so the trees do not grow very tall but are often much older than they look. As the trail winds through the forest you should catch your first glimpses of the ocean after about a mile.

You soon emerge from the forest to cross a 100-yard-long wooden bridge spanning a meadow of salt marsh grass that stretches to the ocean far in the distance. After crossing the bridge you will arrive at Coast Guard Beach. There are awesome views up and down the beach. Low-hanging clouds give a rather mysterious appearance to the ocean as the surf rolls in. These are the same beaches the pilgrims saw as they searched for a place to land in the year 1620. This trail is generally level, and the round-trip distance is 5 miles.

The Cape Cod Rail Trail also originates from the Salt Pond Visitor Center. After a short trip west across U.S. 6 and through several neighborhood streets you reach it. The trail is straight as an arrow and seems to be endless as it fades in the distance. It is lined with 20- to 40-foot pine trees to the left. After about two miles the vegetation thins to your right and allows views of Cape Cod Bay in the distance.

Approaching Rock Harbor the smell of seafood is in the air as local restaurants and stands prepare their specialties. This is a nice spot for lunch or a snack. After a short swing down Rock Harbor Road you are again on the bike path. Even thicker vegetation lines the trail, providing abundant shade on the final leg of your route to Nickerson State Park. Including the portion of the trail through the park, this route is about thirty miles round-trip.

The Head of the Meadow Trail originates from the Head of the Meadow Beaches on the northern part of the Cape. It is a short bikepath of only 4 miles round-trip. Passing through low shrub-like trees you are able to catch only glimpses of the large dunes about half a mile in the distance. This trail takes you through Pilgrim Heights and near the Pilgrim Spring, where the Pilgrims first found fresh water in the new world, before it culminates near the Parabolic Dunes.

The Province Lands Trail is highly recommended as a great escape for the whole family. It loops for about eight miles through some of the best dunes on the cape. Dunes come right up against the bike trail and provide constant surprises; you curiously wonder what could be around the next turn as the trail negotiates itself up, around, down, and sometimes between the large dunes. In places, grasses and shrubs battle the wind and surf to hold the dunes in place.

On a side excursion to Race Point, watch for whales spouting columns of water. Also try the side spur to Herring Cove Beach. From here the mainland can be seen about twenty miles on the horizon, especially on clear days. In completing the loop you will encounter a steep upgrade of about 100 yards, then

The beach stretches for miles along the coast.

quickly swing downhill, and in the blink of an eye be out of the sunny dunes and into the cool shaded Beech Forest. A very enjoyable ride.

Other activities include swimming at several beaches on both the east and west sides of the Cape. Surfing is permitted within the national seashore in waters outside lifeguarded beaches. Both fresh and saltwater fishing are allowed, although a state license is required for freshwater fishing. Nature walks and horseback riding are also quite popular at Cape Cod National Seashore.

4. North Carolina: Cape Hatteras National Seashore

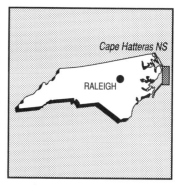

Cape Hatteras National Seashore is located on the Outer Banks of North Carolina. The Outer Banks are a narrow strip of barrier islands, seldom more than a mile wide, that run for about 150 miles off the coast of North Carolina. For thousands of years they have protected North Carolina's mainland from winter storms and tropical hurricanes.

Cape Hatteras was the first of the national seashores, established in 1953. But its history with man begins much earlier. Sir Walter Raleigh tried twice to establish an English settlement on Roanoke Island. The fate of the "Lost Colony," which vanished in 1586, is not known. It is said that Blackbeard met his fate on Ocracoke Island, a place where he often fled to escape his pursuers.

The dunes at Cape Hatteras National Seashore.

29

It is 10:35 on the morning of December 17, 1903. The machine moves slowly forward under its own power and lifts into the air. The flight covers just 120 feet and lasts only 12 seconds, but the Wright Brothers have solved a mystery that has baffled mankind throughout the ages. This flight occurred just north of Cape Hatteras near Kill Devil Hills.

Down through the years, many ships have been lost in the treacherous waters located just off the Outer Banks. The ever-shifting Diamond Shoals, furious winter storms, summer hurricanes, and even war has caused over six hundred ships to run aground or sink. Many wrecks along the shore can be seen to this day.

The bike rides at Cape Hatteras start at different points and traverse very different terrain. The first of two rides begins at

---

Cape Hatteras Lighthouse

Distance: 7 miles, nice family ride

Terrain: Level

Pea Island

Distance: 25 miles

Terrain: Level

Bicycle Rental: Avaialable on Ocracoke Island.

Accommodations: Tourist services are available on all three islands of the seashore. There are five campgrounds in the park. Oregon Inlet, Cape Point, and Ocracoke campgrounds are usually open mid-April to mid-October; Salvo and Frisco campgrounds are usually open mid-June to late August. Campsites may be reserved in the summer through Ticketron. At other times, sites are offered first-come, first-served.

Access: You can reach the seashore from the north via US 17 and 158 or from the west via US 64 and 264. Two toll ferries travel from the mainland to Ocracoke. One leaves from Swanquarter, NC reached via US 264. The other leaves from Cedar Island reached via US 70. Each trip takes about 2 hours. The nearest major airports are located in Wilmington and Raleigh.

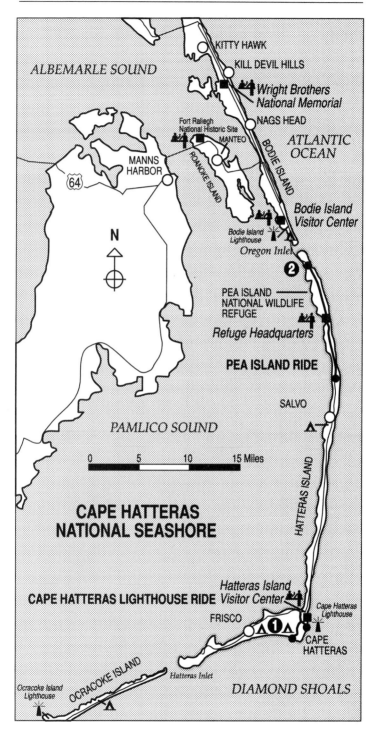

the Hatteras Island Visitor Center under the shadow of the Cape Hatteras Lighthouse. The lighthouse was built in 1870, and at 208 feet is the tallest in the United States.

Take the visitor center road north to Route 12. This road is lined with many marshy areas where you may see white and blue herons. Upon reaching Route 12, double back and head south toward the campground and ocean. Just south of the visitor center the road is lined with loblolly pines. The needles on these trees are very long, at least 8 to 12 inches.

Upon reaching the campground, you can either take the 2-mile loop around the campground, or continue straight for about a quarter mile to the cape to watch waves roll in and to view the Cape Hatteras Lighthouse about two miles down the shoreline. Total round-trip distance is 7 miles over very flat terrain.

The second ride begins at the northern end of Pea Island National Wildlife Refuge. Many species of waterfowl and other birds live in this protected area or stop here during migration. Observation platforms and walking trails allow for closer looks at the bird life. As you head south on this very flat, straight road, you will find salt marsh and ponds to your right with Pamlico Sound in the distance, and high dunes about one hundred yards to the left that block your view of the Atlantic Ocean.

Continuing south past the refuge headquarters, the Pamlico Sound is now much closer on your right, while to the left you are able to catch occasional glimpses of the Atlantic surf between the dunes. Shrubs are more common in this southern area of the refuge. Be prepared for lots of sun during this ride, for there are no trees and thus no shade. Your turnaround point is at the southernmost end of the wildlife refuge. Total round-trip distance is about 25 miles. Try for an early start, because traffic becomes heavy along this road later in the day.

Other activities on Cape Hatteras include sunbathing, beach-combing, and swimming along the shoreline. Sport fishing is popular throughout much of the year, with varying peak periods for different types of fish. Canoeing, sailing, surfing, and snorkeling offer additional opportunities for recreation. And, of course, the Cape Hatteras National Seashore has several campgrounds and nature trails that allow for a first-hand outdoors experience with nature.

5. North Carolina, Tennessee: Great Smoky Mountains National Park

Straddling the border of North Carolina and Tennessee stand the Great Smoky Mountains. These are some of the oldest highlands on earth; geologists estimate their age at over 500 million years. Because of the Smokies' location in the south-eastern United States they were able to escape the glaciers of the last ice age. This has allowed the area to become 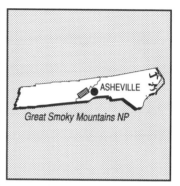 home to a remarkably diverse array of plant life. For instance, within this 800-square-mile national park are found over a hundred species of trees, more than in any other area of similar size in North America.

Deciduous forests grow at elevations generally below 4,500 feet. The tulip poplar may grow to a height of 150 feet or more

and reach a circumference of over 20 feet. Other large deciduous trees include sugar maple, American beech, red hickory, basswood, and magnolia.

Coniferous forests grow at elevations generally above 4,500 feet. Fraser fir and red spruce are the two main components of this high-altitude forest. The red spruce is the larger of the two, sometimes reaching heights of over 100 feet. Fir and spruce grow closely together on the ridges, in many cases their roots intertwined, anchoring them against high winds.

The vegetation everywhere is so varied and lush that the vapor it gives off creates a blue aura or 'smoke,' thus giving

Cades Cove

Distance: 11 miles, nice family ride

Terrain: Generally level, several small hills

Sugarlands

Distance: 60 miles

Terrain: Generally level, surrounding terrain very mountainous

Bicycle Rental: Bicycles can be rented from the ranger station located near the entrance to Cades Cove.

Accommodations: Most neighboring towns have gasoline, food, lodging, showers, and camping supplies. Le Conte Lodge, accessible only by trail, offers accommodations in the park from mid-April to late October. Allow a half day for hiking up a mountain trail to reach this secluded retreat. Rustic hotel accommodations and food service are provided at Wonderland Hotel, in Elkmont, June through October. Additionally, there are ten developed campgrounds in the park that have tent sites, water, fireplaces, tables, and comfort stations. There are no showers or hookups for trailers. Camping is limited to seven days during the summer months. Pickup park handout on bike trails.

Access: From the east, take I-40 to US 19 to US 441 to the park. From the west, take I-40 to Tennessee 66 to US 441 to the park. The closest major airports are located in Asheville, NC and Knoxville, TN.

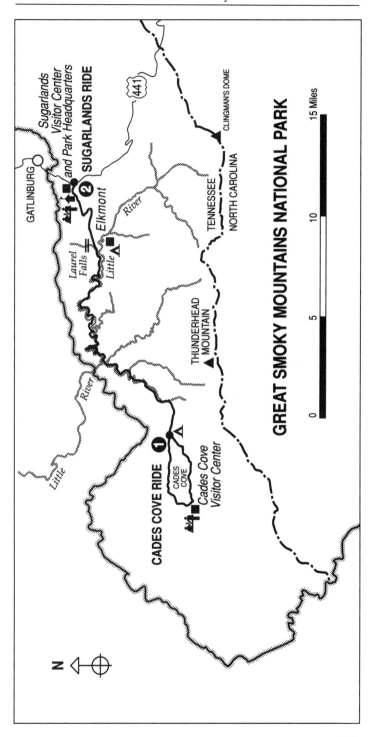

GREAT SMOKY MOUNTAINS NATIONAL PARK

SUGARLANDS RIDE

Sugarlands
Visitor Center
and Park Headquarters

GATLINBURG

Elkmont

Laurel
Falls

Little

Little River

CLINGMAN'S DOME

TENNESSEE

NORTH CAROLINA

THUNDERHEAD
MOUNTAIN

CADES COVE RIDE

CADES
COVE

Cades Cove
Visitor Center

Little River

N

0   5   10   15 Miles

the Smokies their name. The haze that lies almost constantly over the Smokies has its origin in the forested hillsides. The trees exude terpenes, which are hydrocarbon molecules. Sunlight breaks these molecules down; in the process the sun's rays are refracted and the haze is created. The haze is particularly heavy in the fall when large amounts of leaves begin to decay.

The bike rides in the Great Smoky Mountain National Park include a short route excellent for family rides as well as a longer, more challenging route for the avid long-distance cyclist.

The first ride begins at the entrance to Cades Cove. It is an enjoyable family ride that loops for 11 miles through golden sprawling meadows rimmed by green mountainsides in every direction. About one hundred mountain families once lived and tilled their land on this flat valley floor, where some of their rough pioneer houses remain to this day and are open to the public.

If you are able to begin your ride in the early morning, watch for deer browsing in the meadows. This is one of their favorite feeding times. There are also about 400 to 600 black bears in the park, but they are rarely seen.

At about the halfway point of the ride you will reach the Cable Mill, where you can watch the miller grind corn. You can purchase a bag at the nearby Cades Cove Visitor Center.

Continuing on, you enter a more forested area where shade is much more prevalent than on the first half of the route. There are a couple of short, steep hills and sharp blind turns on this 11-mile loop, so be careful, youngsters especially.

The second ride begins at the Sugarlands Visitor Center and follows the Little River Road to and through Cades Cove and back again. The round-trip distance is about 0miles. The route wanders through steep mountainsides where large rock overhangs are quite common. Rhododendron can be seen in bloom during the months of June and July in many places along the road.

Shortly into your ride, the Little River begins to parallel the route and breaks the peaceful silence of the forest with its gushing fury. Watch for "tubers" on the river.

In places along this route, the trees form a canopy over the road so thick that even at midday only a few of the sun's rays break through to speckle the road ahead.

This route is generally flat even though the surrounding terrain is very mountainous. It is well shaded, providing for a cool ride even on the hottest of summer days. However, attempt to begin early, because traffic along this road becomes very heavy around midday and can prove frustrating for the unprepared rider.

Other popular activities include hiking, fishing, and horseback riding. There are over 900 miles of hiking trails ranging

The Smokies as seen from the road between the Sugarlands Visitor Center and Cades Cove.

from short self-guided nature trails to a 70-mile section of the Appalachian Trail that zigzags along the park ridge. Fishing for rainbow and brown trout is allowed all year in many of the park streams. Riding stables are located throughout the park, providing still another enjoyable way to experience the mountains and valleys of the Great Smoky Mountains National Park.

6. Virginia: Shenandoah National Park

Shenandoah National Park is located in the state of Virginia about 70 miles west of the U.S. capital, in a beautiful section of the Appalachian Mountains known as the Blue Ridge. The magnificent Skyline Drive runs the length of the park for approximately 105 miles, offering more than sixty overlooks that provide unforgettable views of the Shenandoah Valley to the west and the rolling Piedmont country to the east.

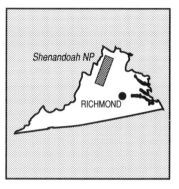

Most of the rocks that form the Blue Ridge are ancient volcanic formations, some exceeding one billion years in age. By comparison, humans have been associated with this land only about 9,000 years. Indians used the land for centuries but left little evidence of their presence.

The Piedmont country of Virginia stretches to the eastern horizon as it is seen from Skyline Drive in Shenandoah National Park.

Settlement of the Shenandoah Valley began soon after the first expedition crossed the Blue Ridge in 1716. By 1800, the lowlands had been settled by farmers, while the rugged mountains were still relatively untouched. Later, as valley farmland became scarce, settlement spread into the mountains. The mountain farmers cleared land, hunted wildlife, and grazed sheep and cattle. By the twentieth century, these people had developed a culture of their own, born from the harshness and isolation of mountain living. However, the forests were shrinking, game animals were disappearing, the thin mountain soil was wearing out, and people were beginning to leave.

In 1926, Congress authorized the establishment of Shenandoah National Park. In dedicating the park in 1936, President Franklin D. Roosevelt initiated a novel experiment in returning an overused area to its original natural beauty. Croplands and pastures soon became overgrown with shrubs, locusts, and pine; these in turn were replaced by oak, hickory, and other trees that make up a mature deciduous (leaf-bearing) forest. Now, more than 95 percent of the park is covered by forests with about a hundred species of trees. The vegetative regeneration has been so complete that in 1976 Congress designated two-fifths of the park as wilderness.

Skyline Drive

Distance: 46 miles

Terrain: Hilly, many gradually graded hills

Bicycle Rental: Available in the towns of Front Royal and Waynesboro.

Accommodations: Accommodations include overnight lodging and restaurants at Skyland Lodge and at Big Meadows Lodge, plus cottages that can be rented at Lewis Mountain. Food service, gift shops, service stations, and facilities for campers such as grocery stores are located at various points along Skyline Drive. There are also four campgrounds and seven picnic areas tucked away along this panoramic route.

Access: From the south, take I-64 to Skyline Drive. From the north, take I-66 to US 340 to Skyline Drive. The closest major airports are located in Richmond, VA and Washington D.C.

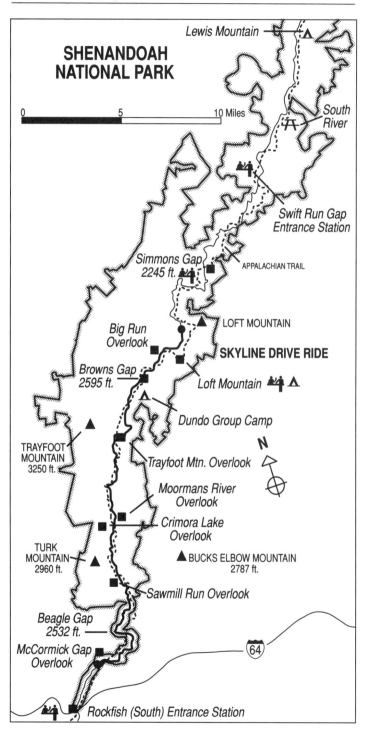

SHENANDOAH NATIONAL PARK

0 5 10 Miles

Lewis Mountain

South River

Swift Run Gap Entrance Station

Simmons Gap 2245 ft.

APPALACHIAN TRAIL

LOFT MOUNTAIN

Big Run Overlook

SKYLINE DRIVE RIDE

Browns Gap 2595 ft.

Loft Mountain

Dundo Group Camp

N

TRAYFOOT MOUNTAIN 3250 ft.

Trayfoot Mtn. Overlook

Moormans River Overlook

Crimora Lake Overlook

TURK MOUNTAIN 2960 ft.

BUCKS ELBOW MOUNTAIN 2787 ft.

Sawmill Run Overlook

Beagle Gap 2532 ft.

McCormick Gap Overlook

64

Rockfish (South) Entrance Station

41

During the summer months the park is alive with many varieties of wildflowers, especially in the Big Meadows area. The park, however, is most popular in the fall when visitors come to view the brilliant colors of the autumn foliage.

The bicycle ride at Shenandoah begins at the Loft Mountain Wayside and covers the southern section of Skyline Drive to the McCormick Gap Overlook. The round-trip distance is 46 miles. This route provides for fantastic panoramic views of the surrounding countryside from many vantage points including seventeen different overlooks along the way. The first, Big Run Overlook, is only about two miles into the ride and allows for a good view of the Shenandoah Valley to the west. At Browns Gap, a strategic location during the Civil War, you are able to view how Stonewall Jackson used the area to enable his amry; to outmaneuver three times as many Union soldiers.

Continuing on, you will find yourself gliding down several runs of a mile or more where, other than for an occasional passing car, the only sounds are those of the wind whistling through the tall trees and of unseen calling birds. On this particular day, I was lucky enough to see two black bears and a hundred or more deer.

As you alternate between pockets of forest and open ridges, you next arrive at Crimora Lake Overlook. The distant farms of the Shenandoah Valley create a beautiful patchwork of tans and greens.

Returning from McCormick Gap, the route gains about00 feet, but it is not at all strenuous. Beagle Gap and Moormans River Overlook provide for excellent views of the rolling Piedmont country to the east.

Other activities include hiking the many trails through- out the park, most of which emanate from Skyline Drive. A 95-mile section of the Appalachian Trail also winds through the park. Fishing for native brook trout provides a challenge in a number of beautiful mountain streams. Camping and picnicking are also quite popular, as well as various campfire and naturalist programs that are led by Shenandoah National Park rangers.

PART II

7. Introduction to the Southern Parks

The parks of the South include Big Bend National Park in Texas, Gulf Islands National Seashore in Mississippi and Florida, Padre Island National Seashore in Texas, and White Sands National Monument in New Mexico.

Big Bend National Park is located in southwest Texas along the Mexican border. The name Big Bend refers to the huge U-turn the Rio Grande makes, forming the 107-mile southern boundary of the park. The park can be thought of as having three natural divisions: the river, the desert, and the mountains. Your bicycle rides at Big Bend experience each of these regions. The Chisos Mountains ride starts out through desert before climbing into the mountains. On this ride you can observe each region's very different forms of plant and animal life. The ride from Castolon, a historic village in the western part of the park, negotiates through the desert country on its way to Santa Elena Canyon and the Rio Grande. The main attractions of Big Bend include the Rio Grande and the three

Sand dunes dominate some of the southern Parks.

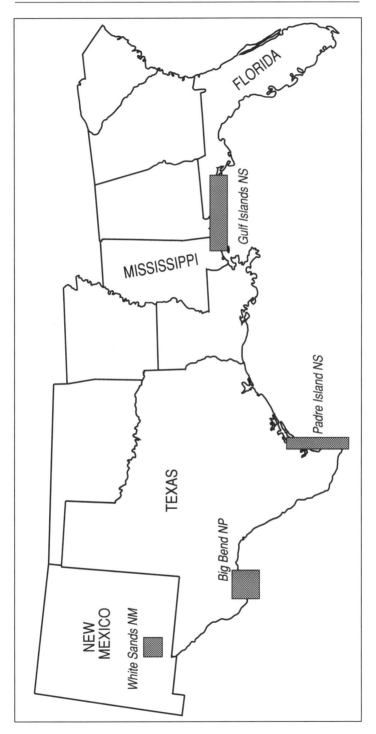

spectacular canyons it has cut; namely, Santa Elena, Mariscal, and Boquillas canyons. The Chisos Mountains, an oasis amidst the Chihuahuan Desert draw many visitors to their heights, and villages such as Castolon provide a sample of the Southwest's history.

The Gulf Islands are barrier islands that help protect the mainland from the direct power of gulf hurricanes. The islands appear to be stationary, but they are slowly moving westward as littoral currents wear away their eastern sides while at the same time building up their western ends. The bicycle rides at the Gulf Islands National Seashore take you past forests of slash pine, old forts and concrete batteries that are now obsolete but remain open for tours, and the beautiful white sand beaches that offer fantastic views of the Gulf Coast shoreline.

Padre Island is one of a chain of barrier islands that stretches along the Atlantic and Gulf coasts of the United States from Maine to Texas. The national seashore of Padre Island is one of the longest stretches of primitive, undeveloped ocean beach in the United States. The bicycle ride at Padre Island National Seashore takes you to and through several of its main attractions. At Malaquite Beach, salty gulf waters roll up onto endless beaches where the only sounds are those of the surf and seabirds. The ride also takes you past the marsh grasslands and tidal flats where a large variety of birds and other wildlife flourish. Near the Grasslands Nature Trail another extraordinary feature of the park may be observed: migratory

sand dunes. Although appearing stable, these dunes move an average of 35 feet per year, and some travel up to 85 feet.

White Sands National Monument is located in south-central New Mexico. It is the largest deposit of gypsum dunes in the world. Many of the dunes are moving to the northeast as much as 20 feet per year, pushed by prevailing southwest winds. The bicycle ramble takes you into the heart of the White Sands with its huge sand dunes. You can see where embryonic dunes have moved on, leaving gypsum pedestals, and where large gypsum dunes must be frequently plowed back in order to keep the loop road open. The Big Dune Nature Trail is a good place to take a hike away from the park road to learn more about the dunes.

8. Texas: Big Bend National Park

Big Bend National Park is located about 300 miles southeast of El Paso, the closest major city. As you can see, the distances here are vast, so be sure to plan accordingly. The name Big Bend refers to the great U-turn the Rio Grande makes here in southwest Texas, forming the 107-mile southern boundary of the park as well as part of the border

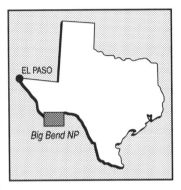

between Texas and Mexico. The river is a ribbon of green strung across the dry desert and cutting through its mountains. As do all rivers that survive desert passages, the Rio Grande has its headwaters outside this desert. The Rio Grande has cut three spectacular canyons within the park: Santa Elena Canyon in the west, Mariscal in the south central, and Boquillas Canyon to the east.

At Big Bend National Park, Texas.

Away from the river floodplain a much more arid world unfolds, for 97 percent of Big Bend National Park is located in the Chihuahua Desert. Arid? Yes. Lifeless? No. Life has simply adapted to minimize expending its energy and to maximize getting, even hoarding water. Some of the adaptations are amazing. The ocotillo develops leaves when it rains, but drops them when it is dry. The creosote bush has roots that produce toxins that discourage the roots of other plants from intruding on their growing space. Creosote bushes that grow along a road tap pavement runoff and may grow twice as tall as those one row back from the road. A prime example of animal adaptation to desert life is the kangaroo rat. It never needs to drink because it can metabolize water from carbohydrates in the seeds it eats. Other animals come out at night when it is cooler, thus requiring less water than they would in the mid-day heat.

Chisos Mountains

Distance: 19 miles

Terrain: Mountainous, several mile ascent and descent

Castolon

Distance: 16 miles

Terrain: Generally level

Bicycle Rental: Bicycles can be rented in the town of Lajitas.

Accommodations: You may find overnight lodging in the park at the Chisos Mountains lodge in the Basin. Campgrounds are located in the Basin, Rio Grande Village, and Castolon. Groceries, cold drinks, camping supplies, and film are sold at the Basin, Rio Grande Village, Castolon, and Panther Junction. Accommodations are also available in Alpine and Marathon, but distances here are vast so be sure to plan accordingly.

Access: From the east, take I-10 or US 90 to US 385 to the park. Approaching from the west, take I-10 or US 90 to Texas 118 to the park. The closest major airports are located in El Paso, Odessa, and Del Rio.

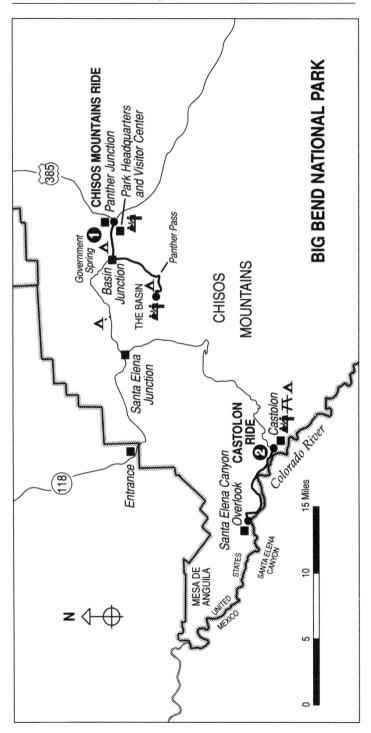

BIG BEND NATIONAL PARK

CHISOS MOUNTAINS RIDE
Panther Junction
Park Headquarters
and Visitor Center
Panther Pass
Government
Spring
Basin
Junction
THE BASIN
CHISOS
MOUNTAINS
Santa Elena
Junction
Castolon
CASTOLON
RIDE
Colorado River
Santa Elena Canyon
Overlook
Entrance
SANTA ELENA
CANYON
MESA DE
ANGUILA
UNITED STATES
MEXICO
N
15 Miles
0   5   10   15

The Chisos Mountains offer an oasis, because of their elevation, from the surrounding desert heat. Even when it may be 100 degrees on the desert floor it is normally at least 20 degrees cooler in the mountains. Rainfall in this region of the park is about twice the amount that falls at Rio Grande Village. Because of the elevation, cooler temperatures, and additional rain, trees such as juniper, pinyon pine, Douglas fir, and ponderosa pine can be found in many places throughout this mountainous section of park.

Prehistoric Indians made their homes here around 6000 B.C. These people were not farmers but hunters and gatherers, taking only what this country offered on its own. Their diet included deer, rabbit, walnuts, prickly pear, and mesquite beans. By 1200 B.C. the La Junta culture dominated. They were desert farmers. During the 1500s the Spaniards enslaved these people and dramatically altered their culture. The Apaches and Comanches both laid claim to this land at differing times. Finally, with the gold discoveries in California the Anglo-Americans began to push in during the 1800s with the presence of military forts and settlements.

Two completely different sections of Big Bend National Park have been selected for bicycle rides. The first ride begins from the Panther Junction Visitor Center located in the heart of the park. Leaving the visitor center, head due west along the main park road toward Basin Junction. To the south the Chisos Mountains, your destination, reach for the sky. It is easy to feel dwarfed in these surroundings, for the distances one can see are immensely vast. Mountains that appear at first to be just ten miles away can easily be fifty or more miles. Fortunately the Chisos Mountains are only five miles to the south.

The first part of the route takes you through true desert. Prickly pear cactus, creosote bush, and ocotillo exist in an extremely parched environment. At Basin Junction you turn south and head straight for the Chisos. Watch for the sotol, a plant of the yucca family that has a large spiny bottom and a straight shoot that extends 10 to 15 feet into the air.

As the road climbs, the vegetation becomes greener and some trees begin to appear along the mountain slopes and ridges. Watch for hawks hunting amidst the spectacular butte formations. In the ravines you may see deer, a favorite food of the park's largest predator, the mountain lion. The Chisos Mountains are prime habitat for the mountain lion, and although the lion is normally found in the backcountry away from roads and people, it may not be a bad idea to pick up a free brochure at the visitor center that explains how you should act should one be encountered.

Above 3,700 feet, oak, juniper, and pinyon pine grow thickly as the road becomes ever steeper. Just after Panther Pass the route makes a very steep descent into the Chisos Basin, your turnaround point. The basin area has a lodge, campground, ranger station, and refreshments.

After an extremely difficult 1-mile ascent out of the basin, the 5-mile marker on the side of the road near Panther Pass signals the beginning of a downhill that will take you all the way back to the main park road. Pedaling is not even necessary for several miles. Carry lots of water for this ride. I drank over 0ounces in just three hours, much more than I normally would for that time and especially that distance. The round-trip mileage is just 19 miles. This ride takes you through an excellent combination of desert and mountain country very difficult to achieve in such a short distance.

The Rio Grande cuts a lush path through an otherwise arid land near Boquillas Canyon in the eastern part of the park.

The second ride emanates from Castolon in the southwestern portion of the park. Castolon, a tiny historic settlement, exemplifies the pioneer way of life the Mexican farmers, U.S. Cavalry, and rugged cattlemen once endured. Again heading west, your destination the Santa Elena Canyon is about eight miles away. High bushes and shrubs that limit your view into the surrounding countryside are common in this part of the park. The huge canyon wall that you can see over the shrubs to the south is in Mexico.

The Rio Grande can first be seen about two miles into this ride. It is a very brown, muddy river that will now parallel your route to the Santa Elena Canyon. The road begins to get a little hillier as you cross washes that are normally dry, but be careful if water is crossing the road, for the currents are swift. This area is also open grazing country for cattle, so do not approach too quickly should you encounter some along or on the road. It is also possible to see roadrunners and jackrabbits in this section of the park.

Soon you reach the Santa Elena Canyon where the Rio Grande seems to disappear between the towering 1,600 to 1,800-foot vertical walls of the canyon. A dramatic climax to this 16-mile round trip adventure. From the nearby picnic area, a footpath leads along a rocky ledge into the heart of the canyon.

Other activities include hiking along short self-guided nature trails located throughout the park and horseback riding in the Chisos Mountains or along parts of the Rio Grande. Rubber raft trips of one, two, or more days along the Rio Grande are also very popular, for a part of the park unfolds to the river-runner that cannot be seen from the road.

9. Mississippi, Florida: Gulf Islands National Seashore

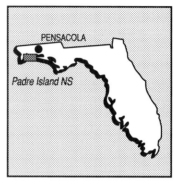

Just off the coast of Mississippi and Florida, amidst beautiful blue gulf waters, white sand beaches, and coastal marsh, can be found the Gulf Islands National Seashore. The seashore stretches from West Ship Island in Mississippi east about 150 miles to Santa Rosa Island in Florida. The Gulf Islands are barrier islands that help to protect the mainland from the direct fury of powerful gulf hurricanes.

The islands appear to be permanent, but they are slowly moving westward as littoral currents wear away their eastern ends while simultaneously building up their western ends. Hurricanes can also make drastic changes to the islands, as Hurricane

Sea oats help to anchor the dunes in place with a root system that can penetrate up to 20 ft deep.

Frederic did in 1979 on Santa Rosa Island, when an entire dune line was pushed clear across the island. On a smaller scale, the wind too affects the islands by constantly reshaping their dunes.

Salt is one of several factors determining the type of plant life found on different parts of the islands. Near the gulf, plants such as sea oats, which are tolerant of high salt levels, can grow. These plants, with their elaborate root systems that penetrate 20 feet below the surface, help to hold the dunes in place. Behind the primary dune, shrubs and trees such as palmetto, slash pine, and scrub live oak can be found, but they never grow much higher than the dunes that protect them from the salt spray. Behind the barrier islands, the waters of the sound and bayou are less salty, and nutrients washed down from the mainland support a rich marine life. Here, shrimp and fish move through many of their life cycles.

When Europeans first arrived on these shores in the early 1500s they reported finding a rich Native American culture. Discovery of this part of the New World was followed by a

---

Fort Pickens

Distance: 5 miles, nice family trail

Terrain: Level

Pensacola Beach

Distance: 15 miles

Terrain: Level

Bicycle Rental: Bicycles can be rented from the campground store near Fort Pickens.

Accommodations: Tourist services are available in the town of Pensacola. Near Fort Pickens, open daily, is a 200 site campground. The campground store has supplies and a laundry. Picnic areas are located near Battery Worth and Battery Langdon. Snack bars may be found at Santa Rosa, Fort Pickens, and Perdido Key.

Access: Take I-10 to I-110 to US 98 to Florida 399 to the seashore. Flights serve the city of Pensacola, which is located just 10 miles to the north.

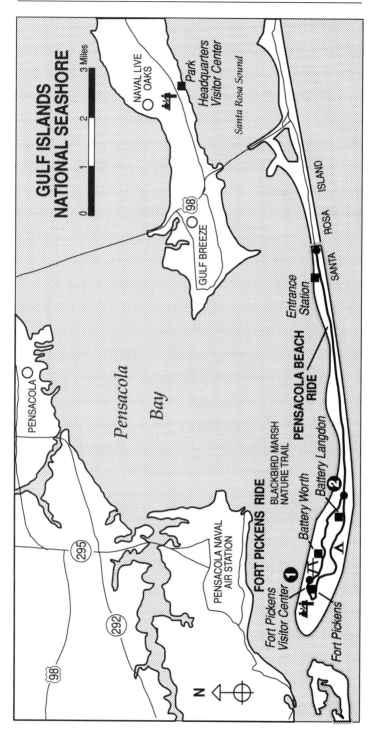

GULF ISLANDS
NATIONAL SEASHORE

0   1   2   3 Miles

NAVAL LIVE
OAKS

Park
Headquarters
Visitor Center

Santa Rosa Sound

98

GULF BREEZE

PENSACOLA

Pensacola
Bay

SANTA ROSA ISLAND

Entrance
Station

PENSACOLA BEACH
RIDE

Battery Langdon

2

BLACKBIRD MARSH
NATURE TRAIL

FORT PICKENS RIDE

Battery Worth

PENSACOLA NAVAL
AIR STATION

295

292

98

Fort Pickens
Visitor Center

1

Fort Pickens

N

55

struggle between colonial powers for its control. Both Spain in the mid-1500s and France about 1700 attempted to establish settlements in present-day Mississippi. The rivalry came to a peak in the early 1800s when the young United States cast acquisitive eyes on this territory. By 1821, the United States had acquired the last of West Florida, and the colonial era ended.

Two different bike routes will be explored at the Gulf Islands National Seashore. The first begins at Fort Pickens, an old military fort whose only action came during the Civil War. The bike trail, excellent for family rides, heads due east through a thick growth of marsh plants, shrubs, bushes, and trees. This trail, upon closer examination, is made not of gravel but of crushed seashell. After a quarter of a mile, there is an excellent view of Fort Pickens on a distant ridge just above the surrounding vegetation. Riding along this part of the trail, you would not know there is a beach and surf less than a mile in either direction. A little farther up the trail, you enter a forest of slash pine, some of which stand on small dunes.

Battery Worth appears next along this route. It is an obsolete military fortification that once housed eight 12-inch mortars. It was completed in 1899 and remained active until 1942. During the 1930s it was essential for army and navy defense activities. Several batteries like this one can also be

White sands along the shores of Santa Rosa Island.

seen on Santa Rosa Island. See the park handout on "Concrete Batteries" for more information.

The route winds briefly through a campground before re-entering the marsh, dunes, and forest just north of Blackbird Marsh Nature Trail, and it continues on for about another mile before culminating near Route 399 and Battery Langdon. The terrain is very flat throughout this trail's 5-mile round- trip.

The second ride continues onto Route 399 and heads east toward Pensacola Beach. Large, crystal-white sand dunes can be seen all around the road. Sea oats grow on many of them. You can hear sea gulls and ocean surf along this road, for a short walk of about 50 to 100 yards puts you right on the white sand beaches of the Gulf Islands.

At the 7-mile mark you've reached the eastern entrance station and the western outskirts of the town of Pensacola Beach. This is the turnaround point, or if you choose, stop off in town for a cold drink or ice cream.

In approaching the Battery Langdon area again, remain on Route 399 rather than retracing your route on the family bike trail you originally came up on. Just past the campground, you enter a forest of slash pine where you can enjoy the unique experience of relaxing and cooling off on a dune under the shade of a pine tree. The terrain on this ride is very flat, providing for an easy ride. This 15-mile round- trip ride passes

Sunset at Shenandoah National Park (see preceding chapter).

numerous white sand dunes and presents many excellent views of the gulf.

Other activities include swimming at the beaches of Ship Horn, Petit Bois, and Santa Rosa islands. Fishing is popular in either the gulf or the waters of the Mississippi or Santa Rosa sounds. Hiking the various nature trails and exploring Fort Pickens or the surrounding military fortifications can be both educational and just plain good exercise. If scuba diving is your interest, ask the park rangers at Fort Pickens where the best places within the Gulf Islands National Seashore are to dive.

10. Texas: Padre Island National Seashore

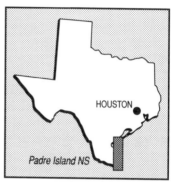

Off the southern tip of Texas, along the Gulf of Mexico just south of Corpus Christi, can be found one of the world's great barrier islands, Padre Island. The island stretches for over 100 miles, protecting the mainland from the violent battering of tropical storms and hurricanes. Running most of its length is Padre Island National Seashore. From the north, only about the first fifteen miles are accessible by car. After this point only four-wheel-drive vehicles can continue on over soft sand beaches into a world little changed over the centuries. The sound of the ocean surf may drown out the sound of your engine.

Along this seemingly endless beach flanked by dunes to the west, behind which lie the grasslands and tidal flats, flourish a large variety of birds and other wildlife. Gulls, great

Looking north from Malaquite Beach, the Gulf waters roll onto the sand.

blue herons, sandpipers, and egrets patrol the shoreline for fish and crustaceans, while birds such as the Eastern meadowlark, sandhill crane, and marsh hawk can be found inland among the dunes and grasslands of Padre Island. In the shallows of Laguna Madre you may see flocks of white pelican searching the waters for fish. Other animals such as the jackrabbit, coyote, and diamondback rattlesnake also inhabit the island. Offshore, various forms of jellyfish abound in the warm gulf waters; the most feared is the Portuguese man-of-war. Armed with long tentacles, it delivers a painful sting with venom 75% as strong as that of the cobra. Luckily, humans rarely receive enough venom to cause any health problems.

Padre Island was the doom of many Spanish galleons sailing this part of the Gulf during the sixteenth and seventeenth centuries. Legends persist of great treasures of gold, silver, and gems hidden and buried along the coast. Some of this wealth has indeed been found; more may be discovered in the future. Current regulations on Padre Island forbid the use of metal detectors as an aid in finding any of these riches hidden in the endless miles of beaches that make up Padre Island National Seashore.

Malaquite Beach

Distance: 25 miles

Terrain: Level, very little shade

Bicycle Rental: Available in Corpus Christi.

Accommodations: Corpus Christi as well as smaller area communities have a variety of visitor services including many that the national seashore does not provide such as lodging, gasoline stations, restaurants, and fishing tackle and bait shops. Inside the park, Malaquite Beach Campground has more that 40 sites suitable for campers with tents or RV's. The campground is open all year on a first-come, first-served basis. Picnic tables, restrooms, cold showers, and a sanitary dump station are provided, however fire grills are not.

Access: From San Antonio, take I-37 to Texas 358 to the seashore. From Houston, take US 59 to US 77 to I-37 to Texas 358 to the seashore. An airport is located in Corpus Christi just northwest of the seashore.

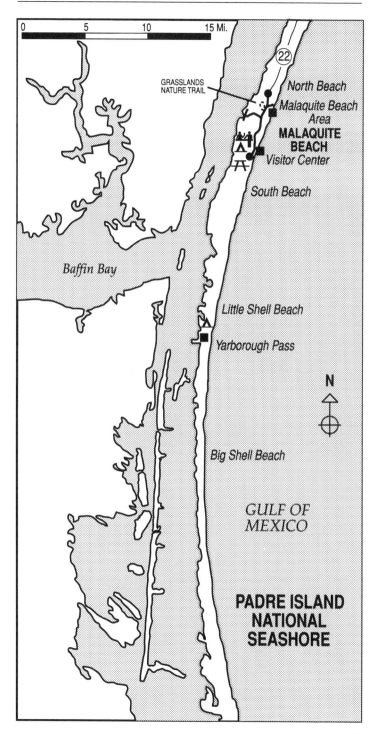

The bike ride at Padre Island begins at the Malaquite Beach Visitor Center. First, head about a mile to the south to reach South Beach for some awesome views of the surf rolling in as far as the eye can see in either direction. The deepening of the gulf water is so gradual that the waves, although not high, seem to roll methodically into the beach for hundreds of feet. Along this beach one may find a shriveling Portuguese man-of-war, but stay away from those tentacles: the stinging cells are still potent. Moving on, head north along the main park road past the Malaquite Beach complex. In this area, you can see high, grass-covered dunes to the gulf side and an endless sea of marsh grass extending to the horizon on the western side of the route. The immensity of the scene dwarfs the sitelines experienced at Cape Cod, Cape Hatteras, and the Gulf Islands. You can hear the ocean surf and many seabirds along this route. Sea oats grow along the ridges of many of the dunes, helping to anchor them in place.

Near the Grasslands Nature Trail you can see the bare faces of migrating sand dunes that are moving across the island. These active dunes are a product of the ever-present winds blowing across the island. The dunes move an average of 35 feet per year, some traveling up to 85 feet.

Continuing on, the pavement becomes rougher about the 7-mile mark as you travel past the north entrance of the seashore. The marsh grasslands and tidal flats continue for mile after mile. Occasional inland sand dunes are generally smaller than the coastal dunes to the gulf side of the road. As you near the northern turnaround point, you can hear the wind rustling through dune grasses, bringing with it the smell of salty gulf waters.

When the park road divides, you have reached the turn-around point of this ride. Turning south, you head into the prevailing southeasterly winds that are extremely refreshing under the hot sun. This is a treeless environment, so be prepared for little shade on this unique 25-mile round-trip ride.

There are many activities to enjoy at Padre Island. Four-wheel-drive vehicles can negotiate the sandy beaches for 60 miles up to the Mansfield Channel. These remote beaches provide for fantastic birdwatching, beachcombing, and hiking. Fishing is an all-season sport on the island. Surf fishermen catch sea trout, redfish, and whiting in the gulf, while flounder can be pulled from Laguna Madre. And, of course, swimming and sunbathing are quite popular on Padre Island National Seashore.

11. New Mexico: White Sands National Monument

White Sands National Monument is located in the Tularosa Basin of south-central New Mexico, about fifteen miles southwest of Alamogordo. At a width of 10 miles and a length of about 30 miles it is the largest deposit of gypsum dunes in the world. Many of these dunes are on the move as prevailing southwest winds push them toward the northeast as much as 20 feet per year.

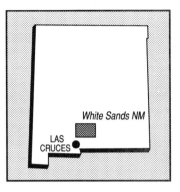

White Sands NM

LAS CRUCES

Created millions of year ago by down-faulting of a huge block of the earth's crust, the Tularosa Basin is surrounded by mountains and highlands. In these mountains, including the forested Sacramentos to the east and the rugged San Andres to the west, are massive layers of gypsum rock. For centuries, waters collecting from seasonal rains and melting snows in

Occasionally, this dune near Big Dune Trail has to be plowed back in order to keep the park road open.

these high ranges have eroded the gypsum deposits. The dissolved gypsum is carried into Lake Lucero, the lowest part of the basin. There the warm sun and dry winds, prevalent much of the year, evaporate the water, leaving a gypsum-crystal- encrusted dry lake bed.

The arid southwest wind persistently scours the bed of Lake Lucero and the alkali flats to the north. Weathering disintegrates the gypsum crystals into sand-size, glistening white grains which are swept away by the wind and added to nearby embryonic sand dunes. As each dune grows and moves farther from the lake and flats, new ones form, rank after rank, in a seemingly endless procession.

The bicycle ride at White Sands National Monument begins at the visitor center located just off the highway. As you leave the center and head into the monument, the large Sacramento Mountains can be seen to your right, and above the dunes to the left rise the San Andres Mountains. Air force fighter planes taking off from the nearby Hollerman Air Force Base periodically rumble overhead.

Park Loop Road

Distance: 15 miles

Terrain: Level, very little shade

Bicycle Rental: Available in the town of Alamogordo.

Accommodations: Tourist services may be found in the town of Alamogordo. Within the monument you may purchase refreshments and souvenirs at the visitor center. A picnic area is located on the 'Heart of Sands Loop Drive' complete with tables, fireplaces, and comfort facilities. Drinking water is available only at the visitor center. There is no campground in the park. A primitive backcountry campsite is available but requires registration and clearance at the park headquarters.

Access: From the east, take I-40 to US 54 to US 70 to the monument. From the south or west, take I-10 to US 70 to the park. From Albuquerque or Santa Fe, take I-25 to US 380 to US 54 to US 70 to the park. The nearest major airports are located in El Paso and Las Cruces.

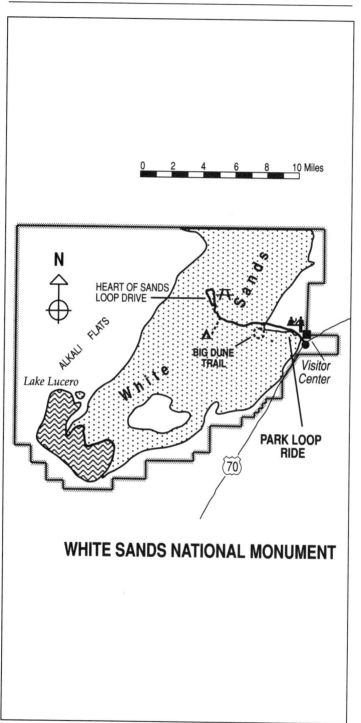

WHITE SANDS NATIONAL MONUMENT

The terrain for the first couple of miles is very flat. The most prominent plant along this section of road is the saltbush. It is a low, grayish shrub very similar in appearance to sagebrush.

At about the 2½-mile mark, a large dune to your left comes right up against the road. This dune must be occasionally plowed back in order to keep the park loop road open. The Big Dune Trail begins near here, where the adventurous hiker can walk among a sea of white sand dunes. A little farther ahead, notice the gypsum pedestals to your right. Plants once grew on top of the dune, and their roots penetrated deep into the sand, binding the grains together. The still-active dune moved on slowly, leaving the columns behind.

At the 5-mile mark of your ride, the pavement ends as you begin traveling on a road of hard-packed gypsum. You are now entering the heart of the White Sands National Monument. In every direction, the sea of gypsum dunes is mesmerizing. Strong bursts of desert wind seem to come out of nowhere, last a couple of seconds, and go. Mile after mile, you move past huge dunes that frequently exceed 50 feet in height. The mountain ranges to the east and west at times cannot be seen, blocked from view by the massive white sands. No vegetation exists in this area, because the dunes are so active it is difficult for any plants to gain a foothold.

As you complete the loop through the heart of the dunes and begin retracing your route along the main park road back to the visitor center, you may find yourself in wonder at what a truly unique bicycle ride this has been. The total round-trip distance is about 15 miles over flat terrain.

Other activities within the monument include hiking and duneclimbing in various areas. Many naturalist-conducted programs are offered during the summer. The park even has a picnic area amidst the heart of the dunes along the loop drive. Photography is best in early evening when shadows create fantastic contrasts among the dunes of White Sands National Monument.

PART III

12. Introduction to the Rocky Mountain Parks

The parks of the Rocky Mountain region include Badlands National Park in South Dakota, Craters of the Moon National Monument in Idaho, Grand Teton National Park in Wyoming, Rocky Mountain National Park in Colorado, and Yellowstone National Park in Wyoming.

The Badlands are located just east of Rapid City and the Black Hills of southwest South Dakota. The pinnacles, spires, and other formations of the Badlands are famous throughout the world as a classic example of erosion on a large scale. The Badlands National Park also contains native grasslands that once stretched from Canada to Mexico and from the Rockies to Indiana, where tens of millions of bison darkened the landscape for miles while they grazed. The Sioux Indians' daily existence revolved around the bison. The way of life they had known for years ended with the bison's extermination.

The bicycle rides in the Badlands take you to such attractions as the Door Trail and Big Badlands Overlook on the

Yellowstone's Lower Falls drop 308 ft. as the river enters the Grand Canyon of the Yellowstone.

northern route. To the west you can visit the Fossil Exhibit Trail, Classic Dikes Overlook, Rainbow Overlook, and the Yellow Mounds. You can visit several prairie dog towns, and everywhere the native grasslands roll to the distant horizon.

Craters of the Moon is a land of lava flows and cinder cones formed when a huge fissure opened in this area about 15,000 years ago. Geologists predict the landscape will erupt again, for the rift zone is only dormant. The bicycle ride takes you through many features of the monument. Along the North Crater Flow Trail you can view many examples of *aa* (very rough) lava and *pahoehoe* (very smooth) lava. From the top of the Inferno Cone you can experience views of the surrounding lava fields that stretch for miles. Just up the loop road is the Big Crater and Spatter Cone. Inside the Spatter Cone you may see snow even in July and August. The Trails to the Tree Molds take you to tree molds that formed when molten lava encased living trees and then hardened. The wood eventually rotted away, leaving the molds. Along the eastern part of the loop ride are the caves. Here you can visit four different caves. You will need a flashlight in all of the caves except Indian Tunnel.

The Grand Tetons dramatically rise above the valley floor of Jackson Hole Basin to form some of the most beautiful mountain scenery in the western United States. The highest peak is the Grand Teton at 13,770 feet, but at least a half dozen neighboring mountains reach heights above 12,000 feet. The Grand Tetons are fault-block mountains that were formed about 9 million years ago when two opposing fault blocks began moving in opposite directions. This process continues today. The bicycle adventure through the Jackson Hole Basin will take you to many beautiful places. You will see the crystal-clear waters of Jenny Lake and the beautiful scenery of the Snake River such as the Oxbow Bend. You will ride for miles through the sagebrush-covered antelope flats where frequent turnouts and overlooks provide incredible views of the Tetons and the Snake River. On the return trip along the Teton Park Road, you will traverse forests of pine and spruce where you can experience even closer views of the Teton range. Another special attraction of the park is its wildlife. Elk, deer, antelope, and bison are quite common. Along the Snake you may see a moose, and there are bighorn sheep in the mountains.

Rocky Mountain National Park is located about sixty miles northwest of Denver. Eighteen peaks rise above 13,000 feet and the highest, Long's Peak, reaches a height of 14,256 feet. Some of the main features of the park include the great U-

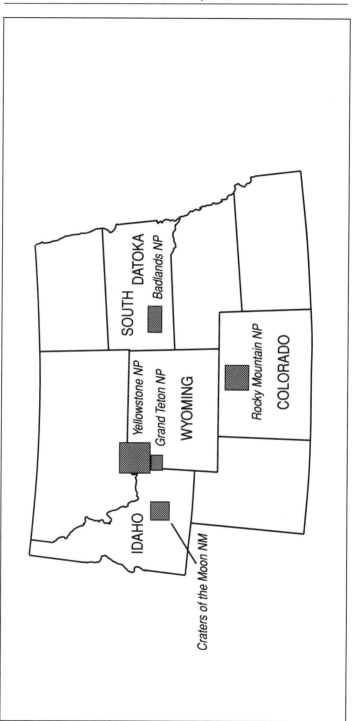

shaped valleys that were formed by the glaciers of the last ice age. Moraines, large ridges of rocky debris that were left by these same glaciers, are also quite common. From Trail Ridge Road, spectacular views of the Rockies stretch in every direction. The Never Summer Mountains can be seen to the west. Another special feature of the park is the transition of vegetation that you can observe during the ride along Trail Ridge Road. In the lower elevations, ponderosa pine and juniper are prevalent. In the higher reaches spruce and fir predominate. Above treeline at 11,000 feet is the alpine tundra, where many of the plants here also grow in the Arctic. Many types of animals live in the park, but the most famous is the bighorn sheep that can be seen along steep rocky ridges or in high mountain meadows.

Yellowstone National Park is located in the northwest corner of Wyoming. It was the country's first national park, established by Congress in 1872. At 2.2 million acres, it is also the largest park of those located in the lower forty-eight states. The park has many spectacular attractions. Along the Upper Loop your bicycle route will pass Mt. Washburn, Tower Falls, Mammoth Hot Springs, Golden Gate, Obsidian Cliff, Roaring Mountain, Norris Geyser Basin where Steamboat Geyser, the world's largest, is located, and the Virginia Cascades. On your route along the Lower Loop, you will ride for miles along the coast of Yellowstone Lake, North America's largest mountain lake. Farther north is the Mud Volcano and the Sulphur Caldron, beyond which you will enter Hayden Valley where the park's many bison frequent. The Upper and Lower falls of the Yellowstone River can be viewed from just south of Canyon. Here, too, is the Grand Canyon of the Yellowstone. It was from this canyon's golden walls that the park got its name. Along the western part of the Lower Loop are the many geyser basins that have made the park famous. Of all the park's many features, the most famous is Old Faithful geyser located in the Upper Geyser Basin. In the southern part of the Lower Loop you will pass through a very mountainous region where the road twice crosses the Continental Divide.

13. South Dakota: Badlands National Park

Located in the rolling grass-lands of South Dakota, about fifty miles east of Rapid City and the Black Hills, is the Bad-lands National Park. The Bad-lands canyons, spires, pinnacles, and ridges are an excellent example of erosion, known the world over. The erosional forces of wind, rain, water, and frost at work today have existed for millions of

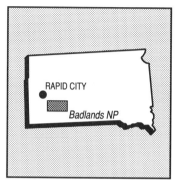

years and will continue to shape the land for millions of years to come.

At the start of the Oligocene epoch about 37 million years ago, this land was a broad marshy plain crossed by slow-moving streams flowing from mountains to the west. Toward the end of this age, volcanoes to the west ejected huge volumes of ash into the atmosphere. Carried eastward by the winds, the

View to the west from the Big Badlands Overlook.

71

ash fell and became the whitish layer near the top of the Badlands formations. Slowly the climate began to change, and increasingly dry winds blew from the north. As rainfall diminished, grass able to grow with less water invaded the drying areas of forest and swampland.

Badlands National Park is a remnant of one of the world's greatest grasslands. From southern Alberta and Saskatchewan almost to Mexico, and from the Rockies to Indiana, prairie grasses covered almost a quarter of the United States. In the moist Mississippi Valley, tallgrass prairie predominated. Westward, as precipitation decreased, the tallgrass gave way to the shortgrass of the High Plains.

The productive prairie sustained herds of bison so vast that they darkened the landscape. By 1890, millions had decreased to not many more than a thousand. Now, in the Sage Creek Basin of the Badlands, bison and the native grasses they browse are carefully protected as surviving elements of a once-vast natural system.

The Oglala Sioux' daily existence revolved around the bison. They not only obtained food from the animal, but shelter and clothing came from the animal's hide, and tools and weapons from the bone. The bison's extermination ended a whole way of life the Indians had known for many, many years.

At first glance, this desolate land seems void of animal life, but many varieties abound. Mule deer can be found in and around wooded draws, and pronghorn antelope, the fastest of North American animals, are quite comfortable in the grasslands. Once vanished from the Badlands, bighorn sheep may occasionally be seen along its ridges. Prairie dogs and coyotes are also quite common throughout the open grassy areas of the park.

There are several bicycle rides to choose from in the Badlands National Park. The first ride heads north from the Ben Rifle Visitor Center at Cedar Pass and quickly enters large spires and ridge formations. The route winds upward through these surroundings and allows for spectacular views of the Badlands to the southeast and the White River beyond. As the road heads back to the west and then north, you enter Cedar Pass, where during the early morning hours the sun creates contrasts between shadow and land that are tremendous. Also, the adjacent dirt mounds that are being gradually washed away by the rains look like chocolate melting.

Farther north, the spires and pinnacles of the Door Trail rise to the right of the road. Past here, the spires are left behind and mounds and flattop erosion is more common, as well as grassland.

The turnaround point for this ride is the Big Badlands Overlook just south of the northeast entrance to the park. This overlook provides an excellent panoramic view of the eastern section of the Badlands. This is a 10-mile round-trip ride.

The second ride heads west from the visitor center over generally flat terrain. You can easily see red-striping in the large spires to the north. You will also observe cottonwood trees and some sagebrush in this area. About four miles into this ride there are very scenic views over the Badlands to the west. Just past the Fossil Exhibit Trail, the spires end and the erosion is again of the flattop variety, with grasslands common especially to the north of the road. This is a 12-mile round-trip ride.

The third ride is really a continuation of the second. Continuing on past the Banded Buttes Overlook, which provides good views of the erosional formations to the south and east, this ride moves through several miles of grassland. The prickly pear cactus is surprisingly common in this section of grassland.

The spires and ridges of the Door Trail resemble paper cut-outs in this scene.

Cedar Pass North

Distance: 10 miles

Terrain: Generally level, one climb and descent

Cedar Pass West

Distance: 12 miles

Terrain: Generally hilly

Yellow Mounds

Distance: 44 miles

Terrain: Generally level, several hills

Needles Highway Loop

Distance: 27 miles

Terrain: Mountainous, some steep, some lengthy climbs and descents

Wildlife Loop Road

Distance: 31 miles

Terrain: Mountainous, some steep, some lengthy climbs and descents

Bicycle Rental: Available in Rapid City and Custer.

Accommodations: Cabins, meals, soft drinks, and other beverages and souvenirs are sold at Cedar Pass Lodge from the beginning of May until mid-October. Accommodations are also available in nearby towns. A campground is located in the western park of the park. Regarding the 'Wildlife Loop Road' and 'The Needles' routes, numerous picnic areas and campgrounds may be found along these highly scenic routes. Various tourist services are also located in surrounding towns.

Access: From the east or west, take I-90 to SD 240 to the park. The closest major airport is located in Rapid City, SD.

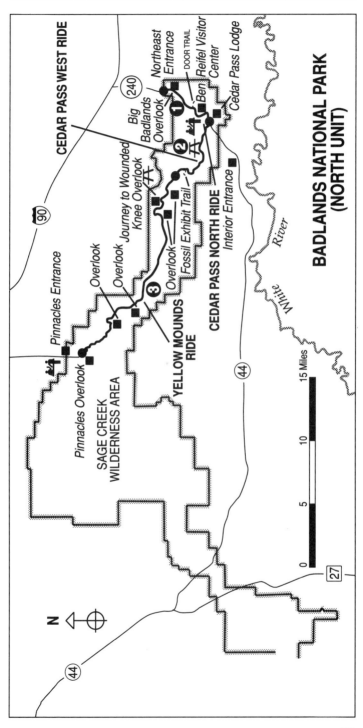

From the Classic Dikes Overlook, you can study the dramatic battle between grasslands and Badlands. The Rainbow Overlook gives you a good observation point to examine the Yellow Mounds area before descending an excellent downhill right into them. From the turnaround point at Pinnacles Overlook, you are able to see the Black Hills far in the distance. This is a 44-mile round-trip ride.

Other activities include hiking on the many self-guided nature trails, joining a park naturalist for an educational evening walk among the Badlands, or visiting an Indian cultural exhibit in the south unit of the Badlands National Park.

The Needles Highway Loop

Located in the Black Hills about fifty miles west of the Badlands are two rides I must tell you about. The first is the Needles Highway Loop. This bicycle ride begins at beautiful Sylvan Lake and heads east into the Needles. The Needles are spectacular rock spires and pinnacles that reach for the sky for about fifteen miles along this road that winds sharply through forests of ponderosa pine. This route provides for many fantastic panoramas of the Black Hills countryside as it climbs and descends the mountaintops. After about seven miles, the road passes through a pretty, grass-carpeted meadow before reentering the forest. You can often see wildlife feeding in meadows such as this. At the south entrance, take 16A west toward Custer. As I made the 1-mile climb up Galena French Creek Divide, I couldn't help noticing the incredible beauty of the dark green pine trees against the blue sky dotted with pure white cotton-puff clouds. A nice downhill will now take you to Route 89, which leads north back to Sylvan Lake to complete this 27-mile loop ride.

Moving northward there are nice views of the Needles in the distance to the east. For the first several miles the road is lined with pretty meadows, in one of which I saw a herd of about fifty bison. As you reenter the forest, you may become aware of the occasional wind that kicks up and roars and howls through the treetops of the tall ponderosa pine forest. If you're from the city, you have to hear it to believe it.

Wildlife Loop Road

This 31-mile loop starts out from the Peter Norbeck Visitor Center located on route 16A. After about a mile, take a right

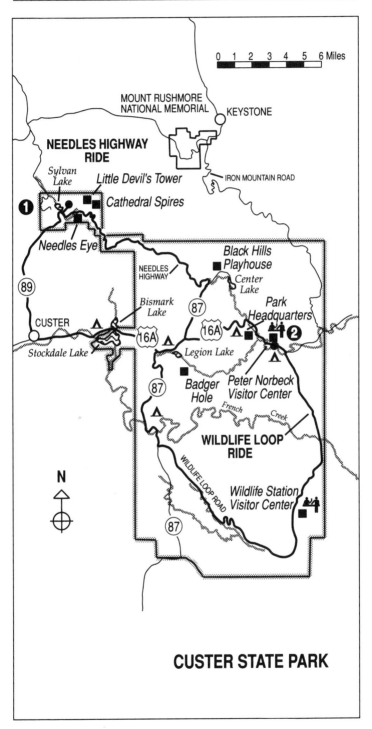

onto the Wildlife Loop Road. The road initially enters a large meadow flanked by pine-covered hills. Just over four miles down the loop road you will enter a small canyon where the forest comes right up to the road.

This route turns west after about ten miles. Right in this area, I saw about ten mules right on the road. A little farther up the road is a prairie dog town where you can observe the pups at work and play. You may also see deer or bison browsing in the adjacent meadows.

Whereas most of the first part of this route seemed to have been on a meadow ridge where I found myself gazing down on the beautiful grassy meadows, the second part of this route traversed a shallow valley where, in turn, I found myself looking up at pine-forested hills and ridges.

After several miles this route ascends through a ponderosa pine forest just before reaching Route 87. Take Route 87 north through a heavily forested area for about four miles, all uphill. After approximately 3½ miles, you will approach a large area destroyed by the 1988 fires. Many burned trees are still standing. In this area there are sensational views to the northeast over the surrounding Black Hills. A little farther up the road, just before beginning a fantastic 7-mile downhill, you can see the Needles to the north. This downhill takes you almost all the way back to the visitor center. The last couple of miles, a small brook meanders along the side of the road.

Nearby attractions in the Black Hills include Wind and Jewel caves, Mount Rushmore National Memorial, Crazy Horse Mountain, and the Black Hills Playhouse. All are easily accessible from Rapid City just 30 miles to the north.

14. Idaho: Craters of the Moon National Monument

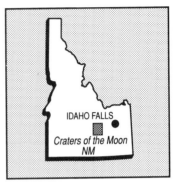

Craters of the Moon is located in south-central Idaho about eighty miles west of Idaho Falls. This is a land of lava flows and cinder cones created when a great fissure in the earth opened about 15,000 years ago. This volcanic activity ceased only 2,000 years ago. Geologists predict the landscape will sometime erupt again, for the rift zone is dormant, not extinct.

Two different types of lava flows intermingle throughout the monument to form this harsh environment. *Aa* lava, pronounced "ah-ah," was more viscous on emerging, which resulted in its very irregular surface that forms an almost impassible terrain to the foot traveler. *Aa* is a Hawaiian term that means unfriendly. *Pahoehoe*, pronounced 'pa-hoy-hoy,' was more fluid on emerg-

Pahoehoe lava flows are seen in the foreground, while the Pioneer Mountains form the background.

ing, and this enabled it to travel longer distances, leaving a relatively smooth surface in a river-like pattern. *Pahoehoe* in Hawaiian means friendly. It is indeed friendly to the hiker, for its smooth surface is very easy to hike across.

It was *pahoehoe* lava that formed the lava tubes and caves that can be found in the eastern part of the monument. When this fluid molten lava flowed out of the ground, it behaved like a stream of water working its way downhill. Soon the surface cooled and hardened. This crust then insulated the molten lava inside, enabling it to keep flowing. The molten lava inside the crust eventually flowed out, leaving the crust as the walls of a lava tube or cave.

This is a land that humans have avoided. Indians hunted here but did not inhabit the area, early western fur trappers went around the lava flows, cattle ranchers stayed away from the place, and miners staked claims only nearby. It has been described by many as a desolate and awful waste.

Within this desolate environment, a great many animals and plants make their home. If you visit the park during early summer, ready yourself for a surprisingly impressive wildflower display when the delicate annuals take advantage of the moisture from the winter snowmelt.

Park Loop Road

Distance: 9 miles

Terrain: Level, one small hill

Bicycle Rental: Available in Sun Valley and Idaho Falls.

Accommodations: Accommodations may be found in towns approaching the monument. Water and restrooms are available at the visitor center and the nearby campground. Take advantage of them here because water is not available anywhere else in the park. Waterless restrooms, however, are provided at the Tree Molds parking lot and at the Cave Area parking lot on the loop road and its spurs.

Access: From the north or south, take I-15 to US 26 to US 20 to the monument. From the west, take I-84 to US 26 to US 20 to the park. The nearest major airports are located in Twin Falls, Pocatello, and Idaho Falls.

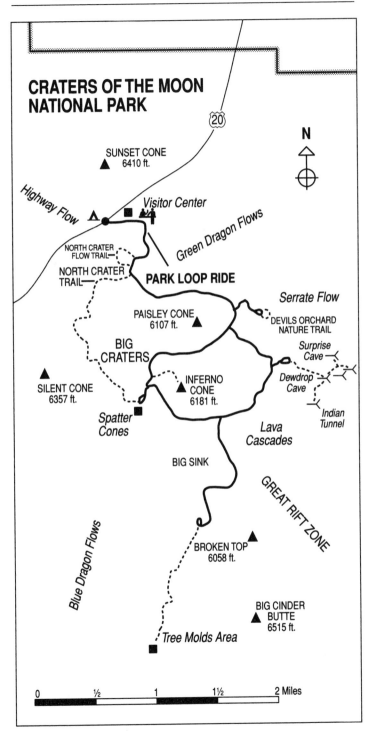

The bicycle ride at Craters of the Moon begins at the visitor center and loops for about 9 miles including a side excursion to the Trails to the Tree Molds area. As you leave the visitor center, *aa* lava flows can be observed just off the road to the right. The black, rust, and green colors of the area provide an unusual aura of beauty. Ahead is the North Crater Flow where you can see excellent examples of *aa* and *pahoehoe* lava.

Advancing on, the bike route skirts the northern side of Paisley Cone. Here, plant life is quite plentiful; trees, shrubs, grasses, and wildflowers can be found all around. This is a common phenomenon along the northern slopes of the cinder cones, because the sunlight is not as direct and thus not as strong as on the southern sides, so the ground retains moisture for longer periods, enabling various plants to flourish.

In the Devils Orchard area, lava bombs are quite common. Lava bombs were formed when airborne blobs of molten lava cooled and hardened as they fell to earth during the eruptions thousands of years ago; the bombs range in length from about an inch to over twelve feet.

Continuing on, you may find yourself appreciating the peacefulness of the area as you pass sagebrush and pine trees fresh with new pinecones. You can hear birds in the distance, but nothing else. Soon, you reach the Inferno Cone. A short climb to the top allows for views of many miles over the

This view of the Big Crater is reached by a short hike from the loop road.

surrounding lava fields. You can easily recognize the chain of cinder cones along the Great Rift. Big Cinder Butte towers above the lava plain in the distance. This is one of the largest purely basaltic cinder cones in the world. From up here, you can readily visualize how the volcanic activity broke out along the Great Rift. Just beyond is the Big Crater and Spatter Cone area. Spatter cones formed along the fissure where clots of pasty lava stuck together when they fell. There is snow inside the cones even on the hottest summer days.

There is a steep 10% grade on this route right after the cone area, but fortunately it is downhill in the direction you are going. A side excursion along a paved road will take you to the Trails to the Tree Molds. Tree molds formed where molten lava flows encased trees and then hardened. The cylindrical molds that remained after the wood rotted away range from a couple of inches to just under three feet in diameter.

The final stop along this route is the cave area. Here, you can explore several lava tubes located about a half mile from the road. You will need a flashlight for all of the caves except Indian Tunnel. The return ride of just over 2 miles to the visitor

Characteristic jagged rocks point to the sky.

center provides excellent views of the soft green Pioneer Mountains to the northwest.

Other activities include ranger-conducted walks and talks held both in the morning and evening. Hiking along the many self-guided nature trails in the monument can be fun as well as educational. Cave exploration in the eastern part of the park can be a very unique experience. For the serious hiker and explorer, the vast Craters of the Moon Wilderness to the south of the park enables long treks across the Great Rift Zone.

15. Wyoming: Grand Teton National Park

Grand Teton National Park is located in the northwest of Wyoming just south of Yellowstone and just north of the town of Jackson. Here on the western side of the Jackson Hole Basin, the Teton range dramatically rises over 7,000 feet above the valley floor, to form some of the most spectacular mountain scenery in the western United States. The

highest peak is the Grand Teton at 13,770 feet, but over a half dozen neighboring mountains reach heights in excess of 12,000 feet.

The Teton range extends for just over 40 miles in length while its width varies from 10 to 15 miles. It is a complete mountain range that was created about 9 million years ago when two opposing fault blocks began moving in opposite

View from the Snake River Overlook.

directions. This process continues today, and also explains the lack of foothills on the range's eastern side.

Wind, water, ice, and glaciers long ago stripped sedimentary layers off the central peaks, uncovering rock nearly as old as the earth itself. Resistant granite, sculpted into the Grand Teton and adjacent peaks, towers as the central range's exposed core. Cascading water cut steep gorges throughout the rising range; the gorges were later widened into U-shaped canyons by huge glaciers that advanced through the gorges and out across the Jackson Hole Basin.

The glaciers have shaped the Tetons more than any other erosional force. Sheer cirque walls, rugged ridges, and jagged peaks reflect the slow dynamic carving by these great masses of moving ice. The massive glaciers also formed many of the beautiful lakes that lie within the park, such as Jenny, Leigh, and Phelps lakes.

In the eastern portion of the park winds the famous Snake River. It originates just south of Yellowstone and flows through the park on its way to joining the mighty Columbia River and the Pacific Ocean beyond. It meanders along beautiful meadows and coniferous forests where abundant wildlife

---

Grand Teton

Distance: 70 miles

Terrain: Generally level, a few hills

Bicycle Rental: Available at Moose, Jenny Lake, Signal Mountain, Colter Bay, and Jackson.

Accommodations: Tourist services are available in the town of Jackson just south of the park. Accommodations are also offered within the park at the following lodges; Jenny Lake, Signal Mountain, Jackson Lake, and Colter Bay Village. Camping is permitted in six park campgrounds. All except Jenny Lake will accommodate trailers and RV's. Campgrounds are operated on a first-come, first-served basis. Three picnic areas are located along this route.

Access: From the south, take US 89, 189, or 191 to the park. From the east, take US 287 or 26 to the park. From the west, take US 26 from Idaho Falls to Idaho 31 to Idaho 33 to Wyoming 22 to US 191 to the park. The nearest airport is just north of the town of Jackson.

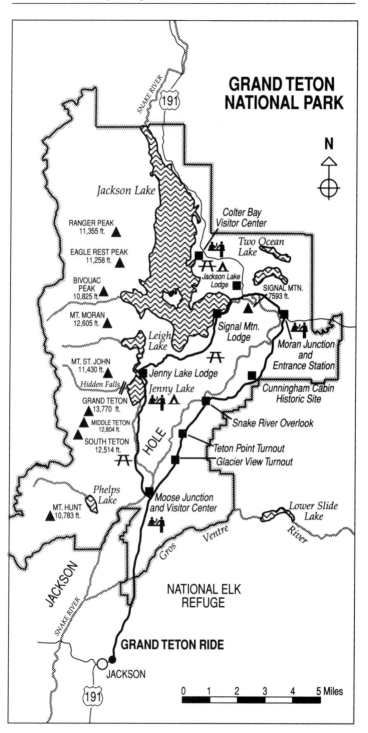

can be seen along its banks and within the surrounding wilderness. Beaver, otter, and trout swim by moose feeding on aquatic plants along the river. Elk, bison, antelope, and deer can be observed throughout the valley.

Indians entered the Jackson Hole Basin about 12,000 years ago. Archeological evidence indicates that small groups repeatedly hunted and gathered plants in the valley from 5,000 to 500 years before the present. Historians credit John Colter as the first white man in the valley, entering in the winter of 1807–08 after breaking away from the Lewis and Clark expedition. Many mountain men followed and trapped beaver. The fur trade era continued until about 1840. Cattlemen and homesteaders followed, but soon found that the short summers hampered farming. Some settlers began dude ranches after realizing that the brutal winters were especially tough on the cattle. Today, Grand Teton National Park is an oasis for many forms of wildlife as well as a recreational wonderland for vacationers seeking an escape from the normal amidst a magnificent mountain setting.

The bicycle ride at Grand Teton National Park begins in the resort town of Jackson. As you head north out of Jackson and through the crisp morning air, the East Gros Ventre Butte blocks your view of the Teton range. Just past the 4- mile mark and up a winding incline, however, there they stand; magnificent or "grand," if you will, against the skyline. The bright rays from the early morning sun shining directly on the mountains bring out sensational color patterns. The dark green of the pine forests, the light green of the meadows, the grays of the granite peaks, the browns of the earth, and the white of the snow and glaciers are simply spectacular.

About six miles into the route you will reach the Gros Ventre River. It begins in the mountains to the east and joins the Snake River about three miles to the west. Many cottonwood trees grow along this crystal-clear, fast-running stream. To the immediate southeast is the National Elk Refuge where during the winter months over 10,000 elk reside. North of the river, the sagebrush flats begin, where you may see antelope, bison, and elk, especially during early morning or evening.

At Moose Junction, continue north along the Rockefeller Parkway, one of the most scenic roads in America. Between the Glacier View Turnout and the Teton Point Turnout, there are many good views of the Snake River winding through a coniferous forest below the elevated sagebrush plain. A little farther ahead at the Snake River Overlook, you can see the river through a border of pine trees as it winds west with the mighty Teton range in full view in the background. A down-hill just beyond will take you past the Cunningham Cabin and through an area of forested meadows.

As I approached Moran Junction, it became apparent that what looked like small hills to the north when I was in the southern part of the park were actually large mountains. At Moran Junction, head west toward Jackson Lake and the Teton Park Road. The Oxbow Bend area is a good place to view wildlife and also provides excellent views of Mt. Moran in the distance.

Heading south along the Teton Park Road, you will pass through marsh and wildflower fields before reaching Jackson Lake for spectacular views of the Tetons across the calm lake waters. Beyond the dam, you enter a wooded area near Signal Mountain Lodge. The forested ridges come right up to the road, temporarily blocking your view of the Tetons. Definitely take the one-way Jenny Lake Scenic Loop. This loop brings you right to the foot of the Tetons and for about one mile follows alongside gorgeous Jenny Lake. South of Jenny Lake,

Mt. Moran stands in the distance across the Oxbow Bend of the Snake River. Skillet Glacier can clearly be seen on its east face.

the route passes through wildflower meadows before reaching Cottonwood Creek.

At Glacier Gulch, you can see the scars left on the Grand Teton by ancient glaciers as they moved down into the valley leaving moraines in front and behind you. Farther ahead, you will pass the fire damage caused by the 1985 Beaver Creek fire before reaching the Moose Visitor Center.

Here, you can either take the Moose/Wilson Road south to 22 and then back into Jackson, or retrace the original route along 191. This is a 70-mile round-trip through magnificent country. It can be shortened to about 45 miles, if you choose, by beginning the loop at the Moose Visitor Center. The Jenny Lake Loop is excellent for family rides. Whatever route or distance you choose, the smells of the sagebrush flats, pine and spruce forests, and campfires, the sights of moose or elk browsing along the river or in a meadow, and of course, the spectacular Teton range, will not easily be forgotten.

The Grand Teton National Park abounds in additional activities for the visitor. Snake River float trips, Jackson Lake cruises, as well as boating, canoeing, swimming and fishing in many of the park lakes and streams are popular water activities. Hiking, backpacking, and horseback riding are some of the more popular land activities. Mountain climbing in the Tetons presents a challenge rivaling the Alps. Those who know are reluctant to rank the Alps above the Tetons in difficulty of ascent. During the winter, cross-country skiing, ice fishing, and sleigh rides into the midst of the elk herd for picture-taking are some of the activities enjoyed by the visitor at Grand Teton National Park.

16. Colorado: Rocky Mountain National Park

Located in the state of Colorado, about sixty miles northwest of Denver and surrounded by national forestlands, is the Rocky Mountain National Park. This is a 'high' land. Its lowest point of about 8,000 feet is near the park headquarters located in the eastern end of the park. Eighteen peaks push their rocky tips above 13,000 feet, and the hig-

hest, Longs Peak, reaches a height of 14,256 feet above sea level. An 8-mile trail leads the well-conditioned hiker to the summit through an array of subalpine forest, alpine tundra, and glacial landscapes. From the summit, the Never Summer Mountains can be seen far to the northwest while in the distance to the east are the Great Plains.

The park road climbs these mountains on its way to the Alpine Visitor Center.

Through a series of upheavals, the mountains were created tens of millions of years ago. Erosional forces have worn away at these highlands ever since, the greatest of which were the massive glaciers of the last ice age that scoured out the U-shaped valleys so prevalent in many parts of the park. Moraines, great ridges of rocky debris that glaciers created along their sides and at their base as they slowly moved along, are also quite common.

Along with the geological features of the park, you can also observe the unique vegetation changes as the elevation increases. In lower regions of the park, ponderosa pine and juniper grow in abundance. Above 9,000 feet, forests of spruce and fir take over. In the upper reaches of the zone the trees become gnarled from the tremendous winter winds that often exceed 150 miles an hour. Above 11,000 feet the trees disappear and the alpine tundra begins. Here, more than a quarter of the plants are also found in the Arctic. The tundra is a harsh world where the growing season is very short, sometimes less than ten weeks. Fragile plants that are five years old may be smaller than the end of one's finger. Extensive damage to the plants in this type of environment may take several hundred years for recovery.

Trail Ridge Road

Distance: 45 miles

Terrain: Mountainous, several hour ascent to Trail Ridge Road

Bicycle Rental: Available at Estes Park and Grand Lake.

Accommodations: Accommodations are available in Estes Park and Grand Lake. There are no motels or hotels in the park. Five park campgrounds—Moraine Park, Glacier Basin, Aspenglen, Longs Peak, and Timber Creek—provide an enjoyable way to become acquainted with Rocky Mountain National Park. Camping is limited to three days at Longs Peak and seven days at the other sites. Many picnic areas are located along US 34 that leads through the park.

Access: From the north or south, take I-25 to US 34 to the park. From the west, take I-70 to Colorado 9 to US 40 to US 34 to the park. The closest major airport is located in Denver.

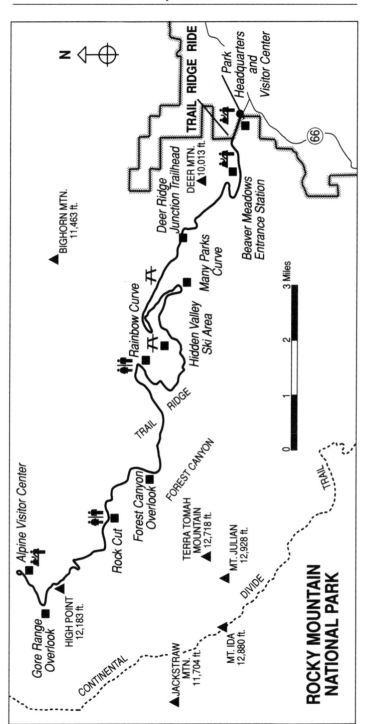

The Continental Divide passes roughly through the center of the park. Precipitation that falls to the east of it will flow to the Gulf of Mexico. Moisture that falls to the west will flow to the Pacific Ocean. The river that carries water westward to the Pacific Ocean is born in the valley just east of the Never Summer Mountains. It is the river that supplies much of the southwest with its fresh water. It is the river that has carved spectacular canyons in Utah and the truly awesome Grand Canyon in Arizona. It is the second longest river in the United States—the Colorado River. It is hard to believe that the small stream flowing out of the park through the Kawuneeche Valley grows into the powerful river that has cut such incredible canyons to the southwest.

Various types of animals may be observed in the park—mule deer, elk, beaver, an occasional black bear, and birds like the hawk and the golden eagle—but the symbol of the Rocky Mountains is the bighorn sheep. Although its range has been greatly reduced from what it once was, the bighorn sheep can still be found along steep rocky ridges or in high mountain meadows.

This bicycle ride begins at the park headquarters located in the eastern end of the park. The road slopes gradually uphill through ponderosa pine and aspen. At Deer Ridge Junction, Trail Ridge Road begins. First opened in 1932, it is the highest continuous paved road in the United States. It follows a route once used by Ute and Arapaho Indians.

The route becomes steeper past Hidden Valley as you climb a mountain ridge at barely more than five miles per hour. Spruce and fir trees have replaced the ponderosa pine that were so common at lower elevations earlier in the ride. At Many Parks Curve after climbing over 1,500 feet, you are able to see moraines formed by ancient glaciers in the forested meadows below. Continuing on up over a ridge and around the mountainside, this route passes through a beautiful spruce forest. Looking to the distant ridge, you can see the road heading upward toward Rainbow Curve.

At Rainbow Curve, more than two miles above sea level, every tree is blasted by wind and ice into distinctive flag shapes; branches survive only on the downwind side of tree trunks. On the farther distant ridge you can see the treeline. You can see several large pockets of snow even though it is the middle of July.

Upon reaching Forest Canyon Overlook, you are now traveling in the alpine tundra where miniature plants and glacier-strewn boulders are the norm and trees are nowhere to be found. At 60 degrees it is warmer than I thought it would be at this elevation. You have climbed over 4,000 feet as you pass Rock Cut and begin a short downhill before starting another steep climb toward High Point. At High Point, the elevation reaches 12,183 feet, the highest point on Trail Ridge Road. It is very windy in this area. On the way back, I took the inside of the road just to be sure a powerful gust of wind wouldn't blow me off the road. Thick, gray clouds literally came out of nowhere and gusted furiously over the ridges in a sight I will not soon forget. The temperature must have dropped at least 10 to 20 degrees as the clouds blocked the sun and the wind chill made it brutal even with sweats and a coat on.

From Gore Range Overlook, you can see the Continental Divide about three miles in the distance. Around a sharp bend in the road appears the Alpine Visitor Center about a mile away, all downhill. This is the turnaround point, and after retracing your path for several miles you are back at Forest Canyon Overlook, where an incredible downhill will take you all the way back to Deer Ridge Junction over ten miles away without pushing a pedal. I had to stop in the sun about halfway down to warm up. My hands were numb from the biting wind, and the bike's handlebars were ice cold. Within just about twenty minutes, in utter contrast, I was soon pedaling through Beaver Meadows in 80-degree warmth, amidst bright sunshine, with my sweats and coat again tucked away in my handlebar bag.

The round-trip distance of this route is about 45 miles. The varying terrain, the steep climb and descent, as well as the spectacular Rocky Mountain scenery make this a truly outstanding ride and an unforgettable experience.

Other activities in Rocky Mountain National Park include hiking one of the many trails within the park. The hiker can choose short half-mile nature trails or long all-day treks to places like Longs Peak. Mountain climbing on the north or east face of Longs Peak presents a demanding challenge for many climbers each year. Horseback riding and fishing are also enjoyed by many a park visitor. During the winter, both downhill skiing at Hidden Valley and cross-country skiing in the lower valleys are very popular activities.

17. Wyoming: Yellowstone National Park

Located in the northwest corner of Wyoming is the gem of the National Park system: Yellowstone. Within its 2.2 million acres can be found North America's largest mountain lake, the world's most extensive geothermal area, and this country's greatest wildlife sanctuary outside of Alaska. It is a place where activity abounds, whether it be a geyser playing in the crisp early morning air or a pair of bear cubs frolicking in an open park meadow.

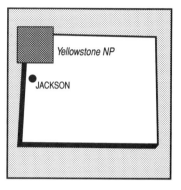

At the heart of Yellowstone's past, present, and future lies volcanism. Several times over the last 2 million years, devastating volcanic eruptions have occurred here. The last eruption, about 600,000 years ago, spewed out nearly 250 cubic miles of debris. This event caused the central portion of the

Steam rises from the hot water seeping from Mammoth Hot Springs on a cool summer morning.

park to collapse, forming a large caldera or basin. The magmatic heat powering those eruptions still powers the park's famous geysers, hot springs, fumaroles, and mud pots. It is generally assumed by geologists that a slowly cooling body of molten rock exists a couple of miles beneath Yellowstone. As rain and snow fall on the park, some of it seeps down in the earth and eventually comes in contact with the heat from this magma. Under enormous pressure, this water is able to be heated to temperatures much higher than the boiling point. The superheated water begins to rise and works its way back to the surface, emerging as one of Yellowstone's thermal wonders.

A hot spring such as Mammoth Hot Springs occurs any time hot, rising thermal water reaches the surface and emerges without being under great pressure. Fumaroles, lacking enough moisture to flow into bubbling pools such as hot springs, vent steam. The steam is often expelled with tremendous force, causing the ground to tremble and producing a strong roaring sound. Mud pots form over fumaroles whose acid gases decompose rocks into mud and clay. Though generally tan in color, mud pots may contain minerals that create shades of gray, black, or red, giving rise to the term 'paint pots.'

The most spectacular thermal features of the park are the geysers. Great quantities of water are stored at tremendous pressure and superheated to a point where a small decrease in pressure causes the hot water to instantly flash to steam. The steam then pushes the remaining water up and out of the geyser tube in a violent eruption. The most famous geyser at Yellowstone is Old Faithful. It plays roughly every hour and reaches heights of over 100 feet. Yellowstone National Park, however, is not all a bubbling cauldron, for the geyser basins cover only a small percentage of the park's land area. In the southeastern portion of the park is Yellowstone Lake, renowned for its excellent trout fishing. This lake is about 20 miles by 15 miles, and its average depth is around 140 feet, 320 feet being its deepest point. From this lake flows the Yellowstone River toward the northern part of the park. Near Canyon Village it surges through the Grand Canyon of the Yellowstone. It is from the towering walls of this canyon that the national park received its name. This area has two great waterfalls. The Upper Falls send the river plummeting 109 feet into a channel of a mile or so before the river cascades over the Lower Falls in a roaring drop of over 300 feet entering the golden canyon.

Most of Yellowstone is composed of pine forest, grass and wildflower prairies, and marshy meadows. Even after the awesome 1988 fires, more than half of the park, including about a million acres of old-growth forest, remains untouched. It is in these areas that wildlife can be observed. In Hayden Valley, elk, moose, and bison are a common sight among the prairie grasses and marshes. Black bears and grizzly bears are normally found in the backcountry, but may occasionally be seen in a meadow near the park road. Bighorn sheep are usually observed in the high country near Mt. Washburn. Mule deer, antelope, and wolves may also be seen in various parts of this huge national park.

The Yellowstone area was discovered by John Colter in 1807 after leaving the Lewis and Clark expedition. His and other early mountain men's descriptions of the park's thermal features were regarded as tall tales. A series of organized government expeditions brought credence to their earlier observations, and in 1872, after much political bickering, the nation's first national park was created by Congress.

The bicycle rides at Yellowstone National Park follow the Grand Loop Road. The first is 70 miles long and negotiates the upper loop, while the second ride, 96 miles, traces the lower loop.

Beginning your first ride out of Canyon Village, head north through lodgepole pine in an uphill path toward Dunraven Pass and Mt. Washburn. At about the 3½-mile mark, there are great views to the east and northeast of the Absaroka range and Beartooth Pass. The Washburn Hot Springs appear as white blemishes in the mountains to the northeast. Just ahead, there are several hillside meadows, in one of which I saw several moose. At Dunraven Pass, I saw a bighorn sheep just off the road on a ledge about twenty feet high.

A downhill begins just after Dunraven Pass and continues to near Antelope Creek. No pedaling is necessary for over five miles. On the way down, you will pass through a couple of miles of fire damaged forest. Severe fire damage can also be seen in the mountains to the northwest just beyond the Pass.

A couple of miles past Antelope Creek you arrive at Tower Falls. Here, the falls drop 132 feet into a smaller section of the Grand Canyon of the Yellowstone. Sheer rock walls of 75 feet or more reach for the sky just to the left of the road, while to the right, rapids thunder in the canyon below.

Along the northern section of this route between Tower and Mammoth hot springs are countless wildflower meadows and beautiful mountain ridges. Two miles past Tower, you will move through another section of trees burned in the 1988 fires. Amidst this blackened forest and in stark contrast to the burned-out trees are beautifully colored wildflowers growing in large abundance.

Continuing on, there is a nice downhill through wildflower meadows as you approach Blacktail Deer Creek. Just before Lava Creek, I saw a coyote wandering alongside the park road. Be sure to stop and see Undine Falls before heading for Mammoth Hot Springs.

At Mammoth Hot Springs, water seeping from the side of a mountain has built spectacular terraces of travertine. The first men to see Minerva Terrace described it as a mountain that had turned itself inside out. Algae give the pools and terrace edges their color. There is an excellent topside view of the hot springs about a mile up the road toward Norris.

Heading toward Norris, the route continues uphill through forested mountain ridges variegated in color and pattern by the 1988 fires. Soon you pass through a steep cliff area void of trees known as the Golden Gate before entering Swan Lake Flat. In this area, I saw a herd of elk numbering at least two to three hundred. Farther up the road, I passed a bachelor herd of bull elk sporting massive racks. Obsidian Creek parallels this route for several miles as you pass through marshy meadows on your way to Obsidian Cliff. Obsidian, a volcanic glass excellent for projectile points and cutting tools, was traded across North America by Indians.

Norris Geyser Basin's array of thermal features is unparalleled. Steamboat Geyser, the world's largest, erupts at irregular intervals of days to years. It reaches heights close to 400 feet, or three times that of Old Faithful. The Porcelain Basin is Yellowstone's hottest exposed area.

Leaving the Norris area, now head east toward Canyon Village to complete the upper loop. Take the Virginia Cascades one-way road to see Virginia Creek as it drops into a deep gorge. Back on the main park road, the route climbs steeply toward the Caldera Rim. Lodgepole pine forest flanks your path on both sides. Beyond the rim, there is a nice downhill taking you back to a meadow just before Canyon where elk frequent.

The second ride begins at the Grant Village Visitor Center and heads north along the shores of Yellowstone Lake toward the Canyon area. Initially there are large sections of forest that had been burned by the 1988 fires, but farther north the forests are green and untouched by the fires. Lookin across the rippling waters of the lake, you can see the snow-capped peaks of the Absaroka range.

In the Fishing Bridge area I saw a bison and several moose right alongside the road. After a nice downhill of a couple of miles, the route begins to parallel the Yellowstone River on its way to the Upper and Lower falls. The Le Hardy Rapids are in this area. Several miles up the road is the Mud Volcano and Sulphur Caldron where you can observe various thermal features of the park. Just beyond, Hayden Valley extends for a few miles to the north along this part of the route. Moose, bison, and an occasional grizzly bear can be viewed in this valley. On this particular day, I saw a herd of several hundred bison grazing in the lower marshy meadow. Fire damage can be seen in the mountains to the north.

Take the side roads to Artist and Inspiration points to get spectacular views of the Grand Canyon of the Yellowstone as well as the 308-foot Lower Falls and 109-foot Upper Falls. Lower Falls is one of the most beautiful waterfalls in the country.

Old Faithful is the world's best-known geyser. Erupting approximately once every sixty minutes, it reaches a height of over 100 ft.

At Canyon Village, turn west toward Norris. Through the tall pine trees, you will be able to see the Gallatin range far to the west. From Norris, the park road heads southwest to Madison as it follows the Gibbon River. Alternating patterns of fire damage are common on the surrounding ridges and mountainsides. Two highlights of this section of your bicycle ride are Beryl Spring and Gibbon Falls.

At Madison you come to the confluence of the Gibbon, Firehole, and Madison rivers. It was near here that a historic campfire meeting took place. Held by the one of the first organized expeditions to survey the park, it was agreed by the expedition members that they would work for legislation to protect this wonderland from exploitation.

Moving on, you will soon arrive at the famous geyser basins. The Lower Geyser Basin features the Fountain Paint Pots as well as Firehole Lake Drive, where you can view the Great Fountain Geyser. A little farther to the south is the

Upper Loop

Distance: 70 miles

Terrain: Generally hilly, one steep climb and descent at Dunraven Pass.

Lower Loop

Distance: 96 miles

Terrain: Generally hilly, mountainous in southern section of Loop.

Bicycle Rental: Available in Rapid City and Custer.

Accommodations: Tourist services are located at Mammoth, Old Faithful, Canyon, Grant Village, Lake Village and Tower. There are many campgrounds throughout the park some of which are Lewis Lake, Bridge Bay, Indian Creek, Norris, and Madison. Over thirty picnic areas may be found along the park's upper and lower loops.

Access: From the south, take US 26, 287, 191, 189, or 89 to the park. From the east, take US 14 or 16 to the park. From the north, take US 89 or 212. From the west, take US 20 or 191 into the park. The closest major airport is located just north of the town of Jackson.

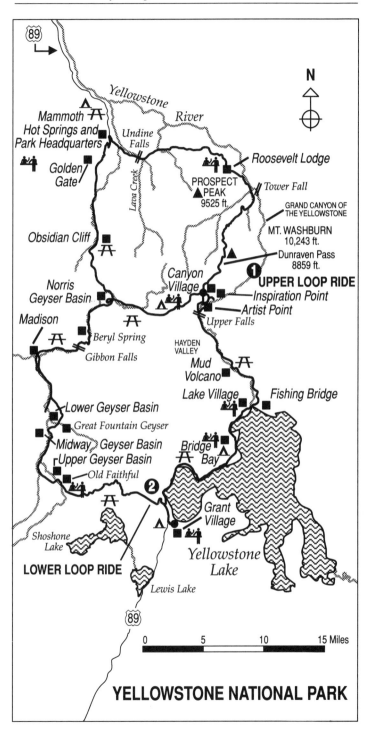

YELLOWSTONE NATIONAL PARK

Midway Geyser Basin, where a short walk takes you to the Grand Prismatic Spring and Excelsior Geyser Crater. Continuing south along fairly level-to-downhill roads, you arrive at the Upper Geyser Basin, where Old Faithful is the main attraction as it faithfully plays approximately every hour. A 1983 earthquake lengthened the eruption intervals from an average of 69 to 76 minutes. The world-famous Old Faithful Inn, a classic log structure saved from the 1988 fires, can also be visited in this area.

Past the Upper Geyser Basin, the route turns more toward the east as you head into some of Yellowstone's high country. Beyond the Kepler Cascades, the park road climbs steeply on its way to the Continental Divide, passing through thick lodgepole pine forest that escaped the 1988 fires. Near the Divide, you can see lily pad ponds along the right side of the road. At Craig Pass you will cross the Divide and begin a 3-mile downhill before climbing to cross the Continental Divide yet again. On the second downhill about a mile before West Thumb, there is a beautiful view of Yellowstone Lake and the Absaroka range beyond.

Allow at least one full day for either of these extraordinary rides. The variety of wildlife, unusual thermal sites, and spectacular scenery of Yellowstone make these bicycle adventures a truly memorable experience.

Other activities in the park include hiking many of the short trails that lead to and through many of Yellowstone's natural splendors. Backpacking and camping in the back- country are also popular. Horseback rides lead from Tower Junction, Canyon Village, and Mammoth Hot Springs into various parts of the park away from the main park road. Boating and fishing can be enjoyed in Yellowstone, Lewis, and Shoshone lakes. And of course, animal-watching and photography are popular pastimes in Yellowstone National Park.

PART IV

18. Introduction to the Southwestern Parks

The parks of the southwest include Bryce Canyon National Park in Utah; Grand Canyon National Park, Petrified Forest National Park, and Saguaro National Monument in Arizona; and Zion National Park in Utah.

Bryce Canyon is a very scenic park. From sunrise to sunset the countless formations are set aglow in fantastic shades of orange and red. The formations have resulted from erosion; the color variations are caused by the different minerals in the rocks. One of the main attractions of the park is the spectacular panorama of the Bryce Amphitheater, which you can best experience from either Fairyland, Sunrise, Sunset, Inspiration, or Bryce points. The other is the Pink Cliffs, best viewed from the Rim Drive that extends along the top of the Pink Cliffs from the Whiteman Bench to Rainbow Point. Here again, various overlooks and points enable beautiful views of some of the park's most impressive formations and scenery.

The parks of the Southwest are known for spectacular views. Here the Grand Canyon.

The Grand Canyon, considered one of the seven wonders of the world, is located in northern Arizona. It is 277 miles long, a mile deep, and up to 18 miles wide. It was formed over millions of years by the Colorado River that now flows deep within the canyon. Some of the key points of interest along the North Rim bicycle ride include the magnificent views into the canyon from the Grand Canyon Lodge, Vista Encantadora, Walhalla Overlook, and Cape Royal. Near Cape Royal, the Cape Royal Nature Trail leads to Angels Window. The South Rim ride takes you past Mather Point, Yaki Point, Grandview Point, Moran Point, and Desert View, where there are excellent views of the inner canyon and the Colorado River. The Tusayan Ruins are archeological sites showing some of the structures that prehistoric people built within the last several thousand years.

The Petrified Forest is located in east-central Arizona. Here logs of petrified wood are now exposed in many parts of the park. The story of man in this region is also readily apparent on the landscape. Sites in several locations tell of the park's human history. Some of the key attractions along the bicycle route through the Petrified Forest include the Painted Desert in the north, the Puerco Indian Ruins and Newspaper Rock where evidence of man's existence in the area can be observed, and of course the petrified wood and logs found at Blue Mesa, Jasper Forest, Crystal Forest, Long Logs, and the Rainbow Forest.

Saguaro National Monument was established to protect the superb stand of giant saguaro cactus found in this part of the Sonoran Desert. This cactus may grow to 50 feet in height and reach an age of 200 years. It provides food for many desert animals and nesting sites for several species of birds. On your rides through this monument you will see not only countless saguaro but several other types of desert plants, such as barrel cactus, prickly pear cactus, creosote bush and ocotillo. The Desert Ecology Trail has information regarding the different plant and animal life to be found. The Cactus Forest Drive and the Bajada Loop Drive give you a real closeness to the land, enabling you to feel part of it.

Zion Canyon has been cut by the Virgin River North Fork, which runs through its length. The canyon walls reach heights in excess of 2,000 feet. Your bicycle ride into Zion will take you to many of its key points of interest. In the eastern part of the canyon is the Great Arch of Zion, a blind arch carved high in a vertical cliff wall. Back in the main canyon you will pass the

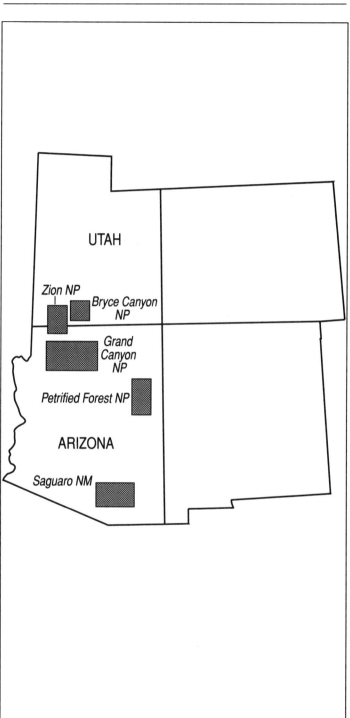

Emerald Pools, Great White Throne, Weeping Rock, and the Temple of Sinawava, where a short trail will lead you to the Gateway to the Narrows. Here, the Virgin River flows through a channel less than 20 feet wide between 2,000-foot canyon walls.

19. Utah: Bryce Canyon National Park

In the south of Utah, about fifty miles east of Cedar City, lies Bryce Canyon National Park. It is a small park as most western national parks go, but its scenic beauty is beyond imagination. From sunrise to sunset the canyon is alive with spectacular shades of orange and red dancing among the countless spires, pinnacles, and hoodoos.

What has powerfully shaped the landscape here is what has also rendered it unusable for most human purposes:

The Red Canyon is located about 10 miles west of Bryce Canyon.

water. What the visitor sees is the product of erosion, and in Bryce Canyon erosion is caused by rain, snow, and ice. Practically all of southwest Utah is in fact a result of the eternal cycle of uplift and erosion. Right now, the land is leading this struggle. This region began rising many millions of years ago until parts of it were more than two miles above sea level. The red rocks here were deposited by vast lakes once covering this area. In earlier times dinosaurs roamed its swamps, eating tons of plant foods; they left their story in fossil bones. The topography in this region rises to the north, creating the Grand Staircase. Descending southward from Bryce Canyon along this staircase, the exposed geological formations become progressively older.

Actually, Bryce Canyon is not a canyon at all, but a huge amphitheater carved by erosion of the 50- to 60-million- year-old rocks of the Pink Cliffs. These cliffs are the uppermost step in the Grand Staircase that rises from the south between the Grand Canyon and Bryce Canyon National Park.

As the elevation at Bryce Canyon changes, so too does its vegetation. As elevation rises from the park boundary out to Rainbow Point, the forest changes from a dwarf forest of

---

Rim Drive

Distance: 40 miles

Terrain: Generally level, one steep climb and descent to the Whiteman Bench.

Bicycle Rental: Available in the town of Rubys Inn, just north of the park.

Accommodations: Cabins are available from May to mid-October at Bryce Canyon Lodge, which has a dining room and gift shop. A general store near Sunrise Point sells film, groceries and souvenirs. Tent and trailer camping is available on a first-come, first-served basis at North and Sunset Campgrounds. Campsites have picnic tables, fireplaces, and nearby water and restrooms. Camping is limited to 14 days. The park has five picnic areas.

Access: From the south, take I-15 to Utah 14 to US 89 to Utah 12 to the park. From Salt Lake City, take I-15 south to Utah 20 to US 89 to Utah 12 to the park. The closest major airport is located in Salt Lake City.

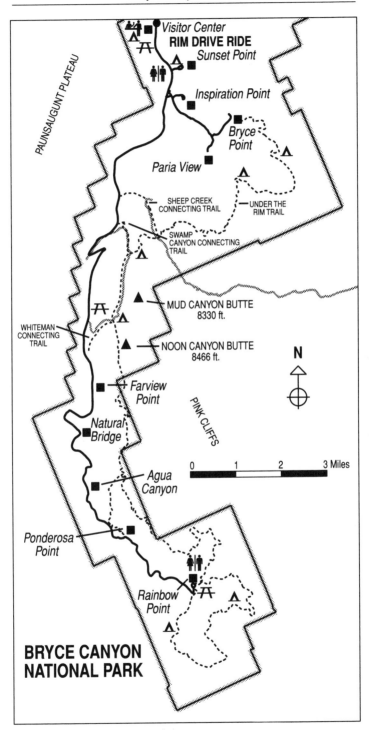

Visitor Center
RIM DRIVE RIDE
Sunset Point

Inspiration Point

Bryce Point

Paria View

PAUNSAUGUNT PLATEAU

SHEEP CREEK
CONNECTING TRAIL

UNDER THE
RIM TRAIL

SWAMP
CANYON CONNECTING
TRAIL

MUD CANYON BUTTE
8330 ft.

WHITEMAN
CONNECTING
TRAIL

NOON CANYON BUTTE
8466 ft.

N

Farview Point

PINK CLIFFS

Natural Bridge

0   1   2   3 Miles

Agua Canyon

Ponderosa Point

Rainbow Point

BRYCE CANYON NATIONAL PARK

juniper and pinyon pine on the lower slopes to ponderosa pine forests on the plateau surface. Even higher up toward Rainbow Point, spruce and fir trees are prevalent. During the summer months, there are beautiful displays of a variety of wildflowers throughout the park's lower meadows.

The forests and meadows of Bryce Canyon support a remarkable diversity of animal life. The smaller animals include ground squirrels, chipmunks, marmots, and mice that feed on seeds and nuts. These animals are preyed upon by fox, coyote, badger, and bobcat. Mule deer are the largest mammals at Bryce Canyon. By browsing on shrubs and young trees along the margin of the forest, they help maintain the meadow environment. They in turn are prey for the very rare cougar. Hunted to near extinction, this animal finds a refuge among the Pink Cliffs.

The cycling excursion at Bryce Canyon follows the Rim Drive where many overlooks, each with a unique view, peer into the rock amphitheater of Bryce. Leaving the visitor center, you will first travel through a ponderosa pine forest. If it is early morning, you can often hear many birds calling in the trees. Within the first fifteen minutes, I observed several deer at different places along this route. Just past the Bryce Point turnoff, the forest opens up to grass and sage meadows rimmed by pine-covered hills. After Swamp Canyon, the road begins a steep ascent to the Whiteman Bench.

It is at the Whiteman Bench that you get your first view into the canyon. The cliffs and formations are set aglow into multi-colored bands and patterns from the early morning sun. The yellows, oranges, and reds are caused by iron oxides in the rocks, the purples and lavenders by manganese.

Along the road I could hardly feel a breeze, but through the upper portions of the pine trees I could hear the rustle of a good breeze. As you continue to climb in elevation, spruce trees begin to appear. From Farview Point, the first turnout you come to, you can see the magnificent orange cliffs of Rainbow Point in the distance. Also, about 75 miles to the northeast the Henry Mountains appear on the horizon in the clear, crisp morning air.

At the next turnout you will get a good view of a large natural bridge in the orange cliffs below. This bridge is 54 feet wide and 95 feet high. Continuing on, the park road winds back through the forest briefly before reaching Aqua Canyon. The early morning sunlight angling through the pine forest away from the canyon is absolutely gorgeous. From the Aqua

Canyon overlook you will be able to see many large spires, one of which is called the Hunter.

To this point, I have seen about fifteen deer. If you're quiet, they will continue to browse right alongside the road, sometimes not more than ten yards away. At the overlooks, brave chipmunks will come right up to your feet looking for food.

Moving on, at Ponderosa Point you can view alternating layers of orange, tan, and white on the canyon walls. The trees far below look like they are the size of a fingernail. As you reach Rainbow Point there are panoramic views to the north and south. The forest has changed from pine to spruce and fir due to the 1,000-foot elevation climb that you have made since

The rock amphitheater of Bryce as seen from Inspiration Point.

leaving the visitor center. These types of trees thrive at higher, cooler elevations.

The rim road is generally flat except for a few small hills. Turning off the rim on your way back at the end of the Whiteman Bench is a nice 2- to 3-mile downhill that brings you back to the ponderosa pines and open meadows.

Before returning to the visitor center, stop off at Inspiration and Bryce points for the most breathtaking views into Bryce Canyon's rock amphitheater that you will find in the park. Absolutely fabulous. The round-trip distance of this unique ride is 40 miles. Definitely take an extra roll of film, as you will find yourself taking more pictures than usual.

Additional activities include hiking on many of the park's self-guided trails including the Under-the-Rim Trail that winds the length of the park to Rainbow Point. Park staff offer campfire programs, rim talks, and nature walks during the summer and fall. Two-hour and half-day horseback riding trips into the canyon leave from the Bryce Canyon Lodge daily. Helicopter flights over Bryce Canyon can be arranged at Ruby's Inn located 6 miles outside the park. Winter activities at Bryce Canyon National Park include cross-country skiing and snowshoeing.

20. Arizona: Grand Canyon National Park

Located in northern Arizona is one of the seven wonders of the world: the Grand Canyon. Its vastness is mind-boggling. It is 277 miles long, a tenth of a mile to 18 miles wide, and, extraordinarily, over one mile deep. This chasm leaves the visitor in utter amazement. The Grand Canyon of the Colorado River is not only awesome in its depth and some in its depth and

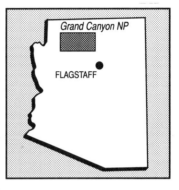

astounding in its extent, but it possesses a dazzling, constantly changing display of colors, light, and shadow that are at their most brilliant during sunrise and sunset.

Deep within the canyon flows the mighty Colorado River. Moving at only a moderate speed, the river can easily carry boulders weighing more than a ton. It is the power of moving water that has created this canyon. Because of the water, wind, gravity, and the energy of expansion and contraction caused by fluctuating temperatures, earth and rock have moved down-

ward to the river, leaving a multitude of smaller canyons behind. The process has taken millions of years, and it is still going on.

Originally, the land through which the Colorado River flowed was flat. However, pressure from within the earth gradually uplifted the surface, causing the river to run faster and cut deeper. Huge amounts of soil and clay were washed away by the powerful currents, creating a deep V-shaped gorge. Canyon walls crumbled from the effects of freezing water, further widening the canyon to its present form. This continuing erosional process may one day leave this land as a plain, much like it was many millions of years ago.

The Grand Canyon is at the bottom of what is known in geologic terms as the Grand Staircase. Being at the bottom, its rocks are the oldest in the series of escarpments that lead from the Kaibab Plateau to the White Cliffs of Zion and on to the Pink Cliffs of Bryce. The black rock known as *Vishnu* Schist, found at the bottom of the inner gorge of the Grand Canyon, is some of the oldest on this planet. It is a staggering 2 billion years old, while the rock along the younger canyon rims is estimated to be 280 million years old.

Various life zones exist throughout the Grand Canyon National Park. Along the rims, the air is much cooler than within the inner canyon, where desert-like plants such as yucca and cactus are common. At the North Rim, spruce and fir forest blanket the land, while at the lower South Rim, ponderosa pine and juniper are more prevalent. Watch for mule deer at the rims and an occasional bighorn sheep among the inner cliffs of the canyon. Hawks and eagles may be seen riding the thermals in search of prey.

The Grand Canyon has been home to people for over 4,000 years. People known as the Anasazi built dwellings of stone and mud, made pottery and stone tools, and farmed. They lived here for over 500 years. In the late 1800s, white men came to mine the minerals and, eventually, to find monetary reward in operating tourist enterprises.

The bicycle adventures at the Grand Canyon consist of rides along both the North and South rims. The North Rim ride leaves the Grand Canyon Lodge and heads north through ponderosa pine. Occasionally, you can see the Bright Angel Canyon between and beyond the trees to the right. Just over a mile up the road, you can see many aspen. At the end of a downhill, you are at Cape Royal Road entering a thick forest of pine, spruce, and aspen that comes right up to the road.

There are sloping hills on both sides as you move gradually uphill. Just past the first picnic area is a nice downhill to the Point Imperial turnoff. Point Imperial is the highest place in the park at 8,803 feet.

Continuing on toward Vista Encantadora, the route becomes very winding with many hills. Large ponderosa pine with diameters of 2 to 3 feet can be seen just off the road, scattered in a thick forest consisting mainly of fir and spruce. An occasional chipmunk may scamper across your path. At Vista Encantadora there are excellent views into the Grand Canyon as well as the Painted Desert beyond. Moving along, however, thick forest blocks the view of the canyon in all but a few places.

As you move temporarily away from the rim and into the forest of Walhalla Plateau, you can see countless pinecones scattered about the forest floor. From Walhalla Overlook to Cape Royal, there are many views of the canyon and the Colorado River far below.

The Cape Royal nature trail has explanations of the many different plants and animals that can be found in this area. This nature trail leads you right up to the Grand Canyon's North Rim walls.

Even with the sun out, the air is cool and refreshing during this ride. There is also a lot of shade along this route because of the mature forest. Ferns can be found in small patches where it is cool and shady. On the way back to the Grand Canyon Lodge, I saw a doe with two fawns about thirty feet from the road. The traffic was light considering it was midafternoon on this 46-mile round-trip ride.

The ride along the South Rim begins from the visitor center in Grand Canyon Village. Heading east, you pass through a forest of pinyon pine and juniper. Yucca is also common on this side of the canyon where it is warmer and drier, which explains the more desert-like vegetation. After about a mile, you will reach Yavapai Point. There are many beautiful, scenic, and breathtaking places in the country, but when you first stand on the rim of the Grand Canyon, there is nothing more awesome than this that I have found anywhere in the country. Absolutely incredible! I think adding to its mystique is the fact that even though it is so huge, you can literally come to within ten or twenty yards of the rim in many places and not even know it is there.

Moving past Mather Point and turning onto the East Rim Drive, you next come to Yaki Point. Here there are good views to the west, north, and east of the surrounding canyon. Looking down into the immense canyon, it is hard to imagine that the inner gorge walls alone exceed 1,500 feet in height. Just beyond Yaki Point, this route passes through a 3-mile-long ponderosa pine forest. Soon, you are again traveling among pinyon pine and juniper. In this area, one can really smell the juniper. After about twelve miles the low forest becomes mixed with deciduous trees.

There is a nice downhill just before the Sinking Ship Overlook; the route along the South Rim has generally been level to this point. From Moran Point, there is a good view of the Colorado River far below, cutting its path through the canyon. Farther ahead, you will reach the Tusayan Ruins. Here there are archeological sites showing some of the structures that prehistoric people built within the last few thousand years. Desert View, this ride's turnaround point, provides the best views of the mighty Colorado River, which through the eons has formed this incredible gorge. The river is muddy brown

---

North Rim

Distance: 46 miles

Terrain: Hilly

South Rim

Distance: 52 miles

Terrain: Generally level, a few gradually graded hills.

Bicycle Rental: Available in Flagstaff.

Accommodations: Complete tourist services are available within the park at Grand Canyon Village, Desert View, and the North Rim. The surrounding towns of Tusayan, Flagstaff, Williams, Jacob Lake, and Fredonia offer many tourist accommodations as well. Campgrounds are located in the Grand Canyon Village, the North Rim, and Desert View. Several picnic areas may be found along each of the rim routes.

Access: From the east or south, take I-40 to US 180 to the South Rim. From the west, take I-40 to Arizona 64 to US 180 to the South Rim. From the north, take US 89 to Alt. 89 to Arizona 67 to the North Rim. The nearest major airport is

---

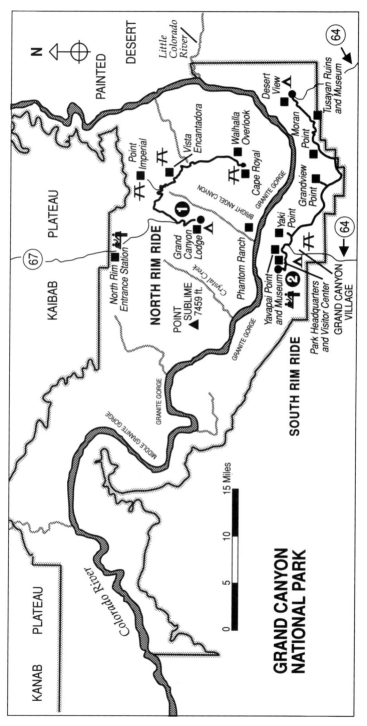

in color as it winds among the steep cliffs and plateaus. Leaving Desert View, the return route is mainly downhill, except for a couple of short hills, for about eight miles to just past Moran Point. Here, the route becomes mainly level all the way back to the visitor center. This side of the canyon has much less shade along the road but is also much more level than the North Rim route. Each of these rides is unique, as are each of the canyon rims they pass through. The round-trip distance of the South Rim ride is 52 miles.

There are many ways to experience the immensity of the canyon. Probably the most common is hiking the Bright Angel Trail or the Kaibab Trail to points along the inner canyon. Many nature trails that are shorter and less strenuous line the canyon rims. Mule trips lead into the canyon from both rims. From the North Rim the mule trips head for Roaring Springs, and from the South Rim, Phantom Ranch is the overnight destination. For the more adventurous, river rafting is very popular. Most trips originate at Lee's Ferry and continue through the park and its many rapids to Diamond Creek in the western section of the canyon. The trips vary in length from seven to eighteen days depending upon the type of craft that is used. Motorized rubber rafts are the quickest, while wooden dories powered by the occupants take much more time. Horseback riding and helicopter flights are other ways for visitors to enjoy themselves as well as view this amazing scenic area within the Grand Canyon National Park.

21. Arizona: Petrified Forest National Park

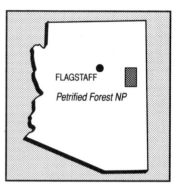

The Petrified Forest National Park is located in east-central Arizona, just south of the huge Navajo Indian reservation and about twenty-five miles east of the town of Holbrook. This park, along with the adjoining Painted Desert, is a land of vast expanses stretching to seemingly endless horizons. On clear days, the San Francisco Mountains over a hundred miles to the west can be seen from the park road.

This high, dry tableland, where only about ten inches of moisture falls per year, was once a vast floodplain crossed by many streams. To the south, tall pine-like trees grew along the headwaters. Dinosaurs and crocodile-like creatures roamed the swamps. The tall trees fell and were washed by swollen streams into the floodplain. There they were covered by silt, mud, and volcanic ash, and this blanket of deposits cut off oxygen and slowed the logs' decay. Gradually, silica-bearing

groundwaters seeped through the logs, and bit by bit, encased the original wood tissues with silica deposits. Slowly the process continued, the silica crystallized into quartz, and the logs were preserved as petrified wood.

After that time, the area sank, was flooded, and was covered with freshwater sediments. Later the area was lifted far above sea level, and this uplift created stresses that cracked the giant logs. Still later, in geologic time, wind and water wore away the gradually accumulated layers of hardened sediments. Now the petrified logs and fossilized animal and plant remains are exposed on the land surface, and the Painted Desert has its present sculpted form.

The story of human occupation in this region is readily seen on the landscape. Sites throughout the park tell of human history in the area for more than 2,000 years. There was a cultural transition from wandering families to settled agricultural villages. Trading ties with neighboring villages developed. Then this story of early people, told by rubble and pictures on the rocks, fades about 1400 A.D. In the mid-1800s, U.S. Army mappers and surveyors came into this area, and soon farmers and ranchers followed. After a period of using the wood as souvenirs, territorial residents recognized that the supply of petrified wood was not endless, and the Petrified Forest National Park was created.

Painted Desert

Distance: 54 miles

Terrain: Generally level, a few gradually graded hills.

Bicycle Rental: Available in Pinetop-Lakeside, Springerville, and Flagstaff.

Accommodations: Food and overnight accommodations may be found in nearby communities such as Holbrook. Services within the park are located at Painted Desert and Rainbow Forest. There are no campgrounds in the park. Only wilderness backpack camping is allowed. Picnic areas are located at Chinde Point and Rainbow Forest.

Access: From the east, take I-40 to US 180 and enter the park from the north entrance. From the west, take I-40 to US 180 at Holbrook and enter the park from the south entrance. The closest major airports are located in Flagstaff and Phoenix.

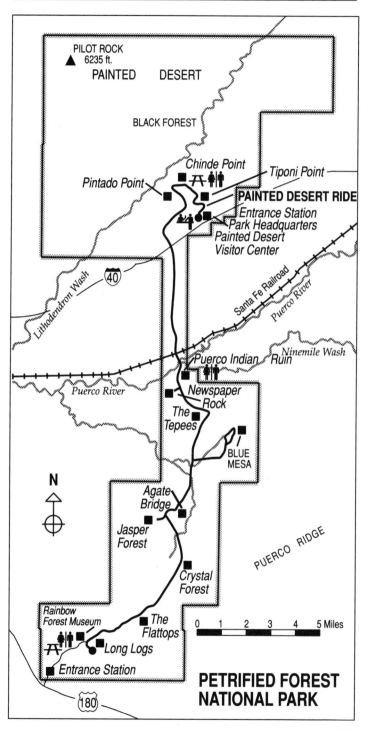

PILOT ROCK
▲ 6235 ft.
PAINTED   DESERT

BLACK FOREST

Chinde Point
Pintado Point
Tiponi Point
PAINTED DESERT RIDE
Entrance Station
Park Headquarters
Painted Desert
Visitor Center

Lithodendron Wash

40

Santa Fe Railroad
Puerco River

Puerco Indian Ruin
Ninemile Wash

Puerco River

Newspaper
Rock
The
Tepees

BLUE
MESA

N

Agate
Bridge

Jasper
Forest

PUERCO RIDGE

Crystal
Forest

Rainbow
Forest Museum
The
Flattops

0 1 2 3 4 5 Miles

Long Logs

Entrance Station

180

**PETRIFIED FOREST
NATIONAL PARK**

The bicycle ride at the Petrified Forest National Park begins at the Painted Desert Visitor Center and follows the park road through the length of the park. Leaving the visitor center, you head northwest through the Painted Desert before swinging around to the south and the Petrified Forest. At Tiponi Point you can see many rust-colored erosional mounds similar to those in the Badlands of South Dakota. Silica fragments cause some of these mounds to glitter in the sunlight. Saltbush, sagebrush, and yucca can be seen in this area as well as throughout most of the park. Trees are very rare.

Petrified logs that have been buried under mud and volcanic ash for millions of years lay exposed in many parts of the park.

In any direction, you will be able to see for great distances. From Pintado Point on clear days the San Francisco Mountains can be seen on the horizon over a hundred miles away. Pilot Rock, the highest point in the park at 6,295 feet, and the Lithodendron Wash can also be observed from this overlook.

Just over the interstate you can see a mountain range far in the distance to the south. Several of the peaks exceed 10,000 feet. Soon you reach the Puerco River, its waters tinged orange-red from the surrounding clay soil. Cottonwood trees, a rare sight in the park, are found along its banks. Next, you will come to the Puerco Indian Ruins, one of the largest ruins in the park. The area was occupied from approximately 1000 to 1300 A.D. Built of stone and masonry walls, the pueblo was once home to a peak population of about seventy-five people.

Continuing on, you next arrive at Newspaper Rock, a huge sandstone block with petroglyphs covering its sides. The terrain in this area is of an olive-tan hue and is very parched in appearance. About two miles up the road, a short downhill will lead you through many cone-shaped hills and erosional formations known as the Tepees. These are colored from iron, manganese, and other minerals. A spur road to the left takes you to Blue Mesa, where pedestal logs abound.

The Agate Bridge is a large petrified tree that crosses a ravine. A cowboy once rode his horse across this to win a $10

The Tepees are found along the park road in the central region of the park. The white layer is sandstone, the dark red layer iron-stained siltstone.

bet. At both the Jasper and Crystal forests, you can see many petrified logs scattered about, some with diameters of 4 feet.

Moving on through the park, there is a downhill from the Flattops to the Long Logs area. Here and at the Rainbow Forest, you can see logs that exceed 170 feet in length. A half-mile foot trail leads through some of the longest petrified logs in the park at Long Logs. Iron, manganese, carbon, and other minerals lend bright colors to the petrified wood. The Rainbow Forest area is a good place to stop and relax before heading north on your return trip. The round-trip distance of the ride is 54 miles through impressively vast country.

Other activities at the Petrified Forest National Park include walking the many self-guided nature trails located at various points of interest along the park road. Wilderness backpacking in the Black Forest or along the Puerco Ridge is enjoyable for those seeking a quiet wilderness experience. Horsepacking is also permitted in the wilderness, but you must provide feed and water for your horses.

22. Arizona: Saguaro National Monument

Located in the southeast portion of the state of Arizona is the Saguaro National Monument. This monument is divided into two sections; the Rincon Mountain unit is about fifteen miles east of Tucson, and the Tucson Mountain unit is located approximately fifteen miles west of the city. Both units are known for their superb stands of the giant saguaro cactus.

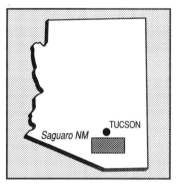

The giant saguaro grows in the desert scrub community, which is found up to about 4,000 feet. Above that is the desert grassland area, then the oak and oak-pine woodlands, the ponderosa pine forest, and on the north slopes below Mica Mountain, the highest point in the monument at 8,666 feet, is a Douglas and white fir forest. These transitional life zones

The Bajada Loop Drive passes ocotillo and saguaro as it curves through the Tucson Mountain unit of the monument.

occur because as the elevation changes, so too do the temperature and precipitation totals.

Only one in a million saguaro seeds may produce a mature plant. By the time the saguaro is about 20 feet tall and has developed its first branch, the remarkable cactus has survived approximately 75 years of desert living. It may ultimately reach a height of 50 feet and an age of 200 years.

A mature plant, weighing several tons, can absorb a great deal of water following the first heavy summer rain. During extended dry periods it gradually uses its stored water, shrinking in girth and decreasing in weight.

Saguaro provide food for countless creatures of the desert. Birds eat the fruits and seeds while they are still on the branches, and many animals, including coyotes, mule deer, and peccaries, eat the fruits after they have ripened and fallen to the ground.

Saguaro also provide nesting sites and protection for several species of birds. The Gila woodpecker and the gilded flicker drill nest holes in the fleshy stems; sap from the exposed

---

Saguaro East

Distance: 8.5 miles, nice family trail.

Terrain: Generally level, a few small hills.

Saguaro West

Distance: 8.5 miles Terrain: Generally level, a few small hills.

Bicycle Rental: Available in Tuscon.

Accommodations: Tourist services are available in Tucson, which is located between the east and west units of the monument. There are no rental accommodations or campgrounds within the monument, but both units have picnic areas in attractive locations.

Access: From the east, take I-10 to Tucson. Take Kolb road north to East Broadway. Go east to Old Spanish Trail to the east unit of the monument. From Phoenix, take I-10 to East Broadway and from there continue as above. To reach the west unit, take Arizona 86 from Tucson west and watch for signs. An airport is located in Tucson.

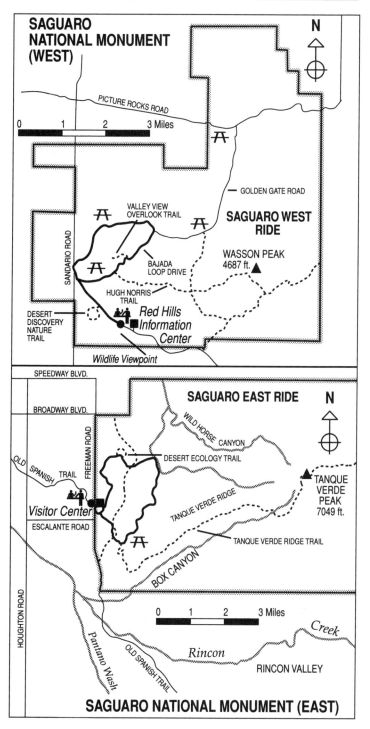

SAGUARO NATIONAL MONUMENT (WEST)

N

0   1   2   3 Miles

PICTURE ROCKS ROAD

GOLDEN GATE ROAD

VALLEY VIEW OVERLOOK TRAIL

SAGUARO WEST RIDE

WASSON PEAK 4687 ft.

SANDARIO ROAD

BAJADA LOOP DRIVE

HUGH NORRIS TRAIL

DESERT DISCOVERY NATURE TRAIL

Red Hills Information Center

Wildlife Viewpoint

SPEEDWAY BLVD.

BROADWAY BLVD.

SAGUARO EAST RIDE

N

WILD HORSE CANYON

DESERT ECOLOGY TRAIL

OLD SPANISH TRAIL

FREEMAN ROAD

TANQUE VERDE PEAK 7049 ft.

Visitor Center

TANQUE VERDE RIDGE

ESCALANTE ROAD

TANQUE VERDE RIDGE TRAIL

HOUGHTON ROAD

BOX CANYON

0   1   2   3 Miles

Creek

Pantano Wash

OLD SPANISH TRAIL

Rincon

RINCON VALLEY

SAGUARO NATIONAL MONUMENT (EAST)

tissue dries and forms a hard lining on the wall of the deep pocket. After the woodpeckers and flickers have raised their young, other birds move in, such as screech owls, flycatchers, and purple martins.

Annual wildflowers in the park are usually at their peak in April. An outstanding wildflower display does not occur every year, for it is dependent on critical amounts of rainfall, sunlight, and warm temperatures at favorable times and intervals. When these conditions are met, the result is one of nature's grandest spectacles. Cacti can bloom even though rainfall has been scarce during winter. In May and early June, creamy-white blossoms appear in clusters on the ends of the saguaro branches.

The first bicycle ride is in the eastern section of the monument. Leaving the visitor center, you head north on a one-way loop road into a cactus paradise. Here are countless prickly pear adorned with red, ripe fruits, barrel cactus, and of course the giant saguaro. This trail is an excellent route for family rides. On your trip, you may hear the hoot of a distant owl or see 5- to 10-inch lizards darting across the trail.

About half of the average rainfall of 11 inches occurs during summer thunderstorms. Such storms can send torrents of water racing down the arroyos. In the winter, storms originating in the Pacific may bring gentle, prolonged rains lasting several days and covering vast regions. Occasionally, a fall hurricane moves northeast from Mexico, causing heavy rains. Large mesquite trees can often be found along the arroyos.

Moving along, you will pass giant saguaro right on the sides of the trail. Creosote bushes are also very common, and when I was here, they were in bloom. The many small yellow flowers attract many bees. So many in fact, that I could hear the constant hum of their wings near these bushes.

As the trail turns east, the Rincon range prominently stands on the eastern side of this section of the park. I strongly recommend you take the side trip along the Desert Ecology Trail. As its name implies, it has excellent information on the plants and animals of the desert.

Continuing on with the smell of mesquite in the morning air, you turn south on the loop road. Here you may see an occasional barrel cactus. Spectacular orange flowers were in bloom on the tops of the barrel cactus I saw this day. Also note how this cactus grows, leaning toward the sun. You can often hear birds along this trail.

At the 5-mile mark, you can see saguaro on the mountain-sides to the east as well as in the valleys to the west. Distant mountain ranges coupled with the saguaro cactus give a truly western flavor to this ride, equivalent to that so common in the old-time western movies.

Several foot-trails lead into the desert wilderness from this loop road. Allow two to three hours to leisurely explore this intriguing desert environment. The round-trip distance is 8½ miles.

The ride in the western section of Saguaro National Monument begins at the information center. As the road heads north toward the Bajada Loop Drive, the vegetation you will pass is

The saguaro cactus can grow to a height of 50 ft. and live to an age of 200 years.

very similar to the eastern unit. Continuing on, you may begin to notice how much more rugged the surrounding landscape is in this section as well as the significantly higher number of saguaro cactus. Ocotillo and cholla are also prevalent in this part of the park.

After about 1½ miles, the road surface changes to a fine gravel road; this is the Bajada Loop Drive. Just past the Hugh Norris Trailhead, the road becomes one-way. Only take this section of the trail if you are an avid bike rider, don't mind leaving a paved road for about one hour, and want to get a real feel for what the Old West might have been like 100 or 200 years ago. Otherwise, don't take this trail—you'll be cursing all the way. Watch for soft spots along the side of the road; they can easily cause a spill. The section between Hugh Trailhead and Golden Gate Road is mainly uphill and very rough. Golden Gate Road is mainly downhill and smoother, with good views to the west.

After 5 miles of gravel road, you will again reach paved road—what a beautiful sight. The round-trip distance in this western unit is also 8½ miles, but don't let the short distance fool you: carry plenty of water.

Other activities include hiking on the short self-guided nature trails as well as backcountry hiking. On a hike from the desert to the crest of the Rincons, you can travel through six distinct plant communities ranging from desert scrub to oak woodland to ponderosa pine to a fir forest near the peaks. Naturalist walks are conducted during the winter months at Saguaro National Monument.

23. Utah: Zion National Park

Located in the southwest corner of Utah, about thirty miles south of Cedar City, is Zion National Park. This is a place of deep, narrow canyons, beautifully colored sheer cliff walls, and incredible rock formations. Winding through the park is the Virgin River North Fork, which millions of years ago created Zion Canyon and one of the park's most popular landmarks, Gateway to the Narrows.

Zion Canyon is incised into the rock of the White Cliffs. The White Cliffs are a middle step in the Grand Staircase, which is a geological formation beginning in the south at the Grand Canyon and ending in the north at Bryce Canyon. Here, the formations range in age from 135 to 165 million years and total more than 2,200 feet in depth. These are the tallest cliffs among

The Great Arch of Zion, as seen from the canyon floor.

the steps of the Grand Staircase. The White Cliffs are really tan in color, but appear white in
sunlight. Their elevation above sea level ranges from 5,000 to 7,000 feet.

The story of Zion Canyon can be summarized into two main parts. Many millions of years ago, changing climates and conditions began laying down sedimentary layers. Sedimentary rocks are formed from materials such as mud or sand that have been moved from a place of origin to a new place of deposition. Most of the sedimentary layers of Zion are either sandstone, shale, or limestone. Zion's most dominant geologic feature, its spectacular Navajo sandstone, consists almost entirely of desert dunes. Following the deposition of these deep sands, seas encroached over the land and carmel limestone was laid down.

The second part of the story is that of erosion. The entire Colorado Plateau has been uplifting and eroding for the last 13 million years, and at this rate, the monuments of Zion may be completely gone in another several million years. Eventually, the rock walls of Zion will tumble and be carried down-

---

Canyon

Distance: 20 miles

Terrain: Generally level, surrounding terrain is very mountainous.

Bicycle Rental: Available in the town of Springdale, just south of the park.

Accommodations: Springdale, Mt. Carmel, and the larger towns of Hurricane, St. George, Cedar City, and Kanab have motels, restaurants, service stations, and grocerystores. Within the park, motel units, cabins, a snack bar, a restaurant, and a gift shop are located at Zion Lodge. Watchman and South campgrounds are open on a first-come, first-served basis. Both have fire grates, picnic tables, water, and restrooms. There are no showers or utility hookups.

Access: From the west, take I-15 to Utah 9 to the park. From the north, take I-15 to Utah 17 and than 9 into the park. From Flagstaff or Phoenix, take US 89 to Utah 9 to the park. The closest major airports are located in Flagstaff, Las Vegas, and Salt Lake City.

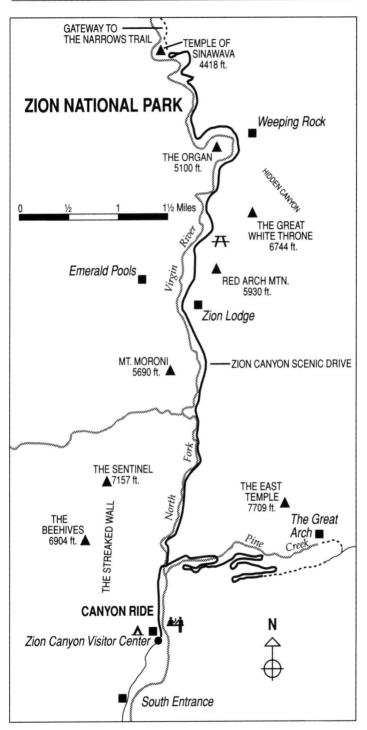

stream by the waters of the Virgin River North Fork. In fact, many of the layers seen in Zion National Park were once also found on top of the Grand Canyon, but they have long since eroded away.

The bicycle journey in Zion National Park begins at Canyon Visitor Center. Leaving the visitor center, head north toward Canyon Scenic Drive. You will find yourself surrounded by huge cliff walls and rock formations of varying shades of pastel color. The Watchman towers to the south, the Beehives and the Sentinel to the northwest, and the East Temple to the northeast. About a mile up the road, this route crosses the Virgin River North Fork and arrives at Canyon Scenic Drive. Before going north, take Route 9 into the eastern canyon to see the Great Arch of Zion, a blind arch carved high in a vertical cliff wall. Enjoy a nice downhill back out to the scenic drive.

Turning north, this route parallels the peaceful Virgin River North Fork where cottonwood, juniper, and prickly pear cactus are plentiful. High up on the cliffs, small juniper and pine seem to grow right out of solid rock.

The 2,000- to 3,000-foot canyon walls, in various shades of red, orange, tan, and white, tower all around as you continue to move farther into this tranquil environment. The quiet and calm of the morning air is compromised only by the waters of the Virgin River North Fork off to your left as it churns among boulders in the riverbed.

The Virgin River North Fork is a river with the looks of a creek and the muscle of the Colorado. This small river almost singlehandedly carved the profound gorge of Zion National Park. It began its downcutting more than 13 million years ago and continues its work today. You may witness the river's power during a flash flood, when it turns muddy and violent, carrying trees and boulders in its raging torrent. But on most days it is a very peaceful river as it winds through the canyon bottom.

The trees thicken as you approach the Zion Lodge. Huge boulders that have at some time in the past broken off from the surrounding cliffs can be seen strewn about the narrow canyon floor. About a mile past the lodge, you can see the Great White Throne, one of the park's most impressive features. Its walls range in color from dark red at its base to bright white at its summit. Continuing on, you will soon reach the Weeping Rock where water that has percolated down through the shale from the highlands emerges along the rock faces and drips in small streams onto the trail and surrounding vegetation. The cliffs just beyond the Weeping Rock come right up

As you travel deeper and deeper into the canyon, the 2,000 ft. walls get closer and closer, until at some points the sheer rock walls literally overhang the road.

to the road. It is easy to see how, long ago, this narrow deep canyon inspired fear in the Paiute Indians, who refused to stay here overnight.

In areas, the rock almost looks as though it were liquid that rapidly solidified; it has the appearance of hardened sand dune. Moving along, the trees again thicken as you approach the Temple of Sinawava and the turnaround point of this ride. From here a popular foot trail leads through towering dark sandstone walls to the Gates of the Narrows. Here, the Virgin River North Fork flows through a channel less than 20 feet wide amidst 2,000-foot canyon walls.

The return trip out of the canyon is generally downhill, and as you ride along, you see and feel the canyon getting wider and brighter. The round-trip distance of this ride is 20 miles.

Other activities include hiking on the many nature trails that lead to such places as the Emerald Pools, the Canyon Overlook, as well as Weeping Rock and the Gateway to the Narrows. Naturalist-led programs frequent these same locations. Longer hikes of a day or more can be made along the canyon rims and through the Narrows. Horseback riding in the backcountry is also a popular activity at Zion National Park.

PART V

24. Introduction to the California Parks

The parks of California include Joshua Tree National Monument, Lassen Volcanic National Park, Point Reyes National Seashore, Redwood National Park, Sequoia National Park, and Yosemite National Park.

Joshua Tree National Monument is located in the Mojave Desert of southern California. In this desert country, extensive stands of joshua trees exist. It is a tree that grows to a height of 40 feet and has thick, woody branches. During the springtime, large white blossoms can be seen on the tips of these branches. Your cycling adventure will take you past the Jumbo Rocks and into Queen Valley where superb stands of joshua trees grow. A hike of 1½ miles will bring you to Ryan Mountain, where you can get sensational views of the monument. In Hidden Valley you can visit a legendary cattle rustlers' hideout while learning about the plants and animals of the Mojave Desert.

California's giant sequoia trees are thought to be the biggest living things —and were the inspiration for the National Parks idea.

Lassen Volcanic National Park was the scene of the most recent volcanic eruption in the forty-eight contiguous states up until the 1980 eruption of Mt. St. Helens in Washington. In 1914, a seven-year cycle of volcanic outbursts, lava flows, mud flows, and a large lateral blast profoundly altered the surrounding landscape. Today a bicycle ride through Lassen will take you through Chaos Jumbles, the Dwarf Forest, the Devastated area, as well as past many thermal features in the southern part of the park. Many beautiful lakes line the park road, such as Manzanita, Reflection, Hat, Summit, Emerald, and Lake Helen. Just north of Lake Helen, a trail leads to the top of Lassen Peak.

Point Reyes is located on a peninsula just north of San Francisco. It is a place of endless sand beaches, steep headlands, quiet meadows, and forested hillsides. It is also a place where two of the earth's great plates grind against each other. Occasionally the results can be devastating, as in 1906. Whereas these plates generally move only several inches per year, in the 1906 San Francisco earthquake the Point Reyes Peninsula was thrust about twenty feet to the northwest. The bicycle rides at Point Reyes will take you to Arch Rock, North Beach, the Sea Lion Overlook, and the Point Reyes Lighthouse. On these rides you will pass through forested glens, open golden park meadows, pastureland, fogbound headlands, and open coastal beaches where the Pacific surf pounds the shoreline.

Redwood National Park is located along the northern coast of California. The tallest trees in the world grow here. Many of them reach heights in excess of 300 feet. Millions of years ago, in a more humid and mild climate, the great redwoods grew over much of North America. They are now restricted to the coastal fog belts of southern Oregon and northern California. Some of the greatest concentrations of redwoods may be viewed at the Tall Trees Grove, Lady Bird Johnson Grove, Big Tree Wayside, and along U.S. 199 in the north of the park. The tallest tree in the world at 368 feet can be visited in the Tall Trees Grove.

Sequoia National Park is the home of the most massive trees on earth. Whereas the redwood of northern California is the tallest, the sequoia is the largest in terms of sheer bulk. Many of the trees are so huge that as many as ten people with their arms outstretched would not be able to encircle their trunks. The bicycle adventure at Sequoia will take you to the Congress Nature Trail where the General Sherman Tree grows, the most massive in the world. In Round Meadow you can see the Puzzle

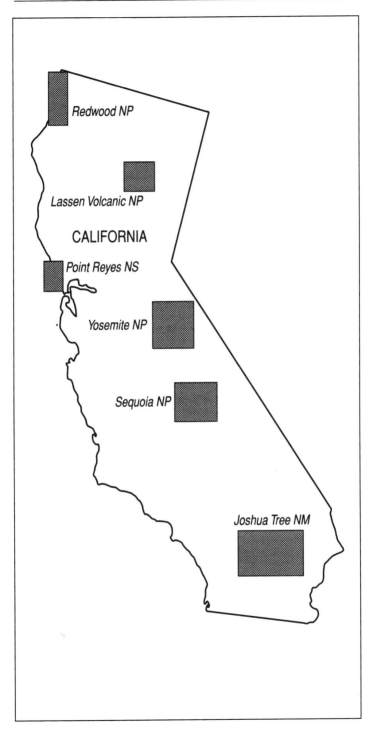

Redwood NP

Lassen Volcanic NP

CALIFORNIA

Point Reyes NS

Yosemite NP

Sequoia NP

Joshua Tree NM

Corner Tree and farther south are the Four Guardsmen and Moro Rock. In the eastern part of the park Mt. Whitney, the highest peak in the continental United States, rears its lofty summit to a height of 14,495 feet.

Yosemite Valley is one of the most beautiful valleys in the world. It is surrounded by towering cliffs shaped by the glaciers of the last ice age. From these sheer granite walls leap half of America's highest waterfalls. On the valley floor, the Merced River flows past open meadows sprinkled with wildflowers, and mixed conifer forests of pine, cedar, and fir. The cycling ramble through the valley takes you past Yosemite Falls, where in two great leaps the Yosemite Creek drops an incredible 2,425 feet. You will pass El Capitan, said to be the largest block of granite in the world at 3,600 feet, and Bridalveil Falls that drops 620 feet. In the eastern part of the valley you will see one of the park's most famous landmarks, Half Dome. The Mariposa Grove of giant sequoia may be visited in the south of the park, and along the Tioga Road spectacular glacier-rounded peaks stretch in every direction. Glacier Point provides amazing views into the valley.

25. California: Joshua Tree National Monument

In the desert country of southern California, about 150 miles east of Los Angeles, is the Joshua Tree National Monument. Here, two large deserts come together, vividly illustrating the contrast between high and low desert. Below 3,000 feet, the Colorado Desert, occupying the eastern half of the monument, is dominated by the abundant creosote bush.

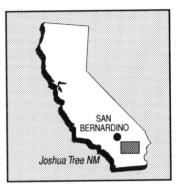

Small stands of ocotillo and jumping cholla cactus can also be seen in this area. The higher, slightly cooler and wetter Mojave Desert is the special habitat of the joshua tree, extensive stands of which grow throughout the western half of the park.

There are several fan palm oases that dot the monument, indicating those few areas where water occurs naturally at or near the surface. Rugged mountains of rock and exposed

granite monoliths testify to the tremendous earth forces that shaped and formed this land.

As old as the desert may look, it is but a temporary phenomenon in the incomprehensible time scale of geology. In more verdant times, one of the southwest's earliest inhabitants, Pinto Man, lived here hunting and gathering along a slow-moving river that ran through the now-dry Pinto Basin. Later, Indians traveled through this area in time with harvests of pinyon nuts, mesquite beans, acorns, and cactus fruit, leaving behind rock paintings and pottery ollas as reminders of their passing.

In the 1800s, explorers, cattlemen, and miners came to the desert. They built dams to create water tanks and dug up and tunneled the earth in search of gold. The Lost Horse and Desert Queen mines and the Desert Queen Ranch are remnants of what they left behind. In the 1930s, home-steaders came seeking free land and the chance to start new lives. Today, many people come to the monument to experience its peace and tranquility as well as open space and clean air.

Within this seemingly forbidden land, a great variety of animal life exists. Rabbits, rodents, lizards, and snakes are food for the larger hunters such as the golden eagle, burrowing owl, bobcat, and coyote. A roadrunner may occasionally be seen. In

---

Jumbo Rocks

Distance: 40 miles

Terrain: Generally level, several gradually graded hills.

Bicycle Rental: Available in Twentynine Palms.

Accommodations: Motels, gas stations, stores, and restaurants are available in nearby towns such as Joshua Tree and Twentynine Palms. Nine campgrounds, with tables, fireplaces, and bathrooms are located throughout the park. You do need to bring water and firewood. Several picnic areas can be found along your route through Joshua Tree.

Access: From Los Angeles, take I-10 to California 62 to the monument. From the east, take I-10 straight to the park. The closest major airports are located in San Bernardino and Palm Springs.

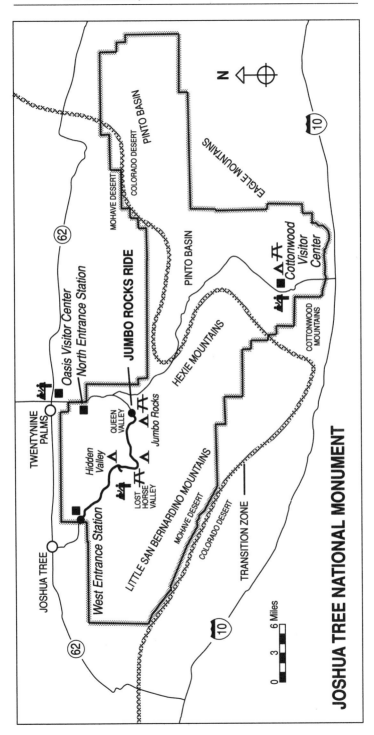

JOSHUA TREE NATIONAL MONUMENT

the higher mountain country, about two hundred bighorn sheep make Joshua Tree National Monument their home.

The bicycle ride at Joshua Tree begins at one of the picnic areas near Jumbo Rocks, about ten miles south of the Oasis Visitor Center. You head west toward Hidden Valley in a gradual climb through beautifully rounded rock formations. Juniper appear near the Jumbo Rocks area and just as quickly disappear. As you enter Queen Valley, you can see joshua trees all around; many offer shade along the road. This tree is found in only the arid lands of the southwest, mainly California. It grows to a height of 10 to 40 feet and during the springtime huge white blossoms grow on the tips of their thick, woody branches.

Moving on, creosote bushes are also common in this desert environment. The surrounding hills, home to the desert bighorn sheep, are brownish and barren in appearance, as if scorched by the relentless desert sun. The route begins to wind downhill for several miles near Ryan Mountain, where you once again pass through many rounded rock formations.

The route turns northward at Lost Horse Valley and heads toward Hidden Valley and the west entrance station. Thomas

The joshua tree, which is only found in the desert lands of the Southwest, can reach a height of 40 ft.

Mountain looms in the distance to the west over the closer Little San Bernadino Mountains. Just past Hidden Valley, a legendary cattle rustlers' hideout, the road again winds gradually downhill for a couple of miles. Many joshua trees grow along both sides of the road as you near the turnaround point. Countless rock monoliths, some right by the road, provide many picture-taking opportunities. Most of the bushes along this route appear very dry, as they await the next rare summer rain.

This is a unique bicycle tour through a harsh desert environment, and it is very different from many of the other rides at various parks and monuments throughout the country. There is very little grass, and no coniferous or deciduous trees grow anywhere in this dry, sandy terrain. Instead, desert vegetation such as the ocotillo, cholla cactus, creosote bush, and of course, the joshua tree grow. Many animals mentioned earlier inhabit this land. So what appears desolate and deserted at first is actually a thriving life zone; it is simply different from what most of us are used to.

A great downhill for the last 2 miles of the monument brings you to the west entrance station and the turnaround point. From here, there are very beautiful views of the surrounding valleys and mountains. The round-trip distance of this ride is about 40 miles. Get an early morning start to avoid

hot afternoon temperatures, common during the summer months.

Other activities include hiking along both backcountry trails as well as the shorter self-guided nature trails along the main park road. Ranger-led walks and campfire talks are conducted during the spring and fall. Camping is also very popular at any of the many campgrounds that are found throughout Joshua Tree National Monument.

26. California: Lassen Volcanic National Park

Located in the rolling ever-green forests of north-central California, about fifty miles east of the town of Redding, is Lassen Volcanic National Park. Until the 1980 eruption of Mt. St. Helens in Washington, Lassen Peak was the most recent volcanic eruption in the contiguous forty-eight states. It was in May of 1914 when the peak began a seven-year cycle of sporadic volcanic outbursts. During this cycle, lava flows, mudflows, and a huge lateral blast profoundly altered the surrounding landscape.

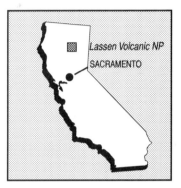

Lassen Peak is the southernmost volcano in the Cascade range, which extends from here into Canada. The western part of the park features great lava pinnacles, huge mountains created by lava flows, jagged craters, and steaming sulphur

Scientists think that Lassen Peak is one of the most likely mountains to join Mt. St. Helens and become an active volcano.

vents. It is cut by spectacular glaciated canyons and is dotted and threaded by lakes and rushing clear streams. Snowbanks persist year-round, and beautiful meadows are spread with wildflowers in spring. The eastern part of the park is a vast lava plateau more than one mile above sea level. Here are found small cinder cones such as Crater Butte and Fairfield Peak. Forested with pine and fir, this area is studded with small lakes, but boasts few streams.

On an even grander scale, Lassen Peak is but one of many active, dormant, or extinct volcanoes that extend around the Pacific Ocean in a great 'ring of fire.' This zone of volcanoes and earthquakes marks the edges of plates that compose the earth's crust. Volcanic and seismic disturbances occur as these great slabs override or grind past each other.

The theory of plate tectonics holds that as the expanding oceanic crust is thrust beneath the continental plate margins, it penetrates deep enough into the earth to be partly remelted. Pockets of molten rock or magma result. These become the feeding chambers for volcanoes such as Lassen Peak, as well as Mt. Shasta, Mt. Hood, and Mt. Rainier.

The Lassen area was a meeting point for the Yana, Yahi, Maidu, and Atsugewi Indians. Because of its weather and snow conditions, generally high elevation, and its seasonally

---

Manzanita Lake

Distance: 26 miles

Terrain: Generally hilly, several long ascents and descents.

Bicycle Rental: Available from the campground store at Manzanita Lake.

Accommodations: Tourist accommodations are available in Redding, Red Bluff, Mineral, Chester, and Susanville. Within the park there are seven campgrounds that operate on a first-come, first-served basis. Five of these are located right on the park road while two are found in the back-country. Four picnic areas are also situated along the park road.

Access: From the south, take I-5 to California 36 to California 89 to the park. From the north, take I-5 to California 44 to the park. From the east, take I-80 to California 89 to the park. The closest major airports are located in either Reno or Sacramento.

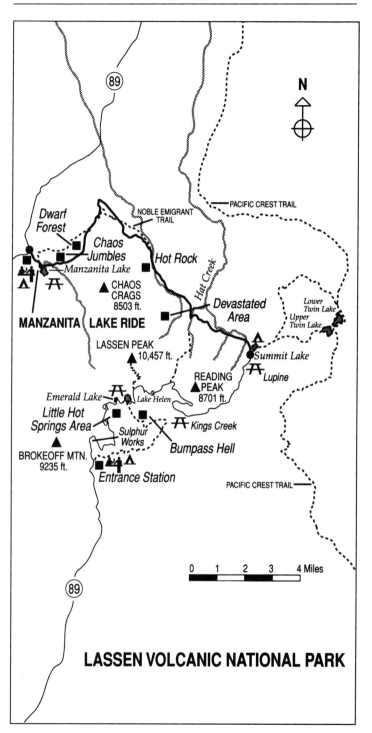

mobile deer populations, the Lassen area was not conducive to year-round living. These Indian groups encamped here in warmer months for hunting and gathering. Basketmakers rather than potters, they have left few artifacts other than stone points and knives.

History here generally describes the period from 1840 on, even though mountain man Jedediah Smith passed through in 1828 on his overland trek to the West Coast. California's gold rush in 1848 brought the first settlers. Two pioneer trails, developed by William Nobles and Peter Lassen, are associated with the park. In 1851, Nobles discovered an alternate route to California passing through Lassen. Sections of this Nobles Emigrant Trail are still visible in the park. Lassen, for whom the park is named, guided settlers near here and tried to found a city. Mining, power development projects, ranching, and timbering were all attempted here.

Your bicycle adventure at Lassen begins at the Manzanita Lake Visitor Center. Heading east, you will first climb uphill through well-established pine and fir forest. Many of the trees reach heights of 100 to 150 feet. Birds can be heard calling from the trees and large volcanic rocks litter the forest floor while to your right are beautiful evergreen- covered mountains. Just past the west entrance, you can see Manzanita Lake to the right. A small gravel turnout brings you down to the shoreline. Across the lake, Lassen Peak looms in the distance still clad in places with the previous winter's snow.

Continuing on, Reflection Lake is to the left, a good place for trout fishing. Soon you enter the Dwarf Forest and Chaos Jumbles, where violent steam explosions from the base of the Crags caused avalanches that resulted in this huge area of volcanic debris. Many coniferous trees grow within this debris, but to heights of only 10 to 20 feet, earning the name of the Dwarf Forest. This area extends for about two miles before you enter a large spruce forest where the trees reach heights of 100 to 200 feet. An excellent downhill takes you through this forest for just over two miles. About halfway down there are spectacular views to the east as pine- and spruce-covered mountain ridges retreat to the far horizon. This descent culminates near the Crags campground.

Moving now in a southeasterly direction, your route soon parallels the Lost Creek. It was here and at Hat Creek where mudflows raged through the valleys in 1915. Hot Rock, a 300-ton piece of lava that was carried five miles down the mountainside in one of these flows, got its name because it was still hissing forty hours later. It can be seen right off the road in this area. Also near here, many huge pine trees grow, some with diameters of 4 to 5 feet. There are also several huge stumps extending about 10 to 20 feet into the air, all that remains after the incredible lateral blast blew and snapped their tops right off.

Near the 9-mile mark, Lassen Peak towers to the right and a high cliffside is a couple hundred yards to the left of the road. Patches of aspen trees dot the coniferous forest. Just up the road is a turnout with a short history on the eruption of 1915. Farther along, you will arrive at Hat Creek as it winds through a pretty meadow with evergreen ridges as a backdrop. Beyond Hat Creek, you enter a thick spruce forest where most trees exceed 100 feet in height. The final section of the ride to Summit Lake is a steep uphill. The Summit Lake area with its adjacent campground is a good place to stop for lunch before returning to Manzanita Lake. The round-trip distance of this ride is 26 miles. The southern section of Lassen Volcanic National Park, not covered by this ride, is also a beautiful area to cycle. You can observe many thermal lakes from along the park road.

Other activities include camping, hiking the many trails, and horseback riding. Boating and fishing are popular on many of the park's lakes and streams. During the winter, 400

Lake Helen is a nice spot to stop for a picnic.

to 700 inches of snow falls on the park, enabling winter sports enthusiasts to enjoy the landscape. Near the south entrance, downhill skiing is offered; cross-country skiing is popular in the northwest part of the park near Manzanita Lake.

27. California: Point Reyes National Seashore

Point Reyes National Seashore is located just thirty miles northwest of San Francisco on a triangular piece of land that juts out into the waters of the Pacific Ocean. Often fog-bound, especially in summer, it is a place of thundering surf that rolls in along miles of endless sand beach and steep headlands. Away from the coast, the fog thins, the air warms, and you can experience quieter, more serene sights of pastureland, meadows, and forested hills.

The Point Reyes Peninsula is an unusual, dislocated land that long baffled geologists. Why should the rocks of this craggy coast match those of the Tehachapi Mountains? The answer lies in continental drift. The peninsula rides high on the eastern edge of the Pacific plate. This, one of the six great

Looking south from Arch Rock, the surf rolls in against steep headlands.

plates forming most of the earth's crust, creeps steadily north-westward about three inches a year. The rest of North America, except Alaska, is borne westward on the slower-moving American plate.

In Olema Valley, these two great land masses grind together. Where one plate ends and another begins cannot be pinpointed accurately, for a single fault line does not exist. This meeting of the plates is simply a rift zone, which contains many large and small faults running parallel and at odd angles to one another. Because each plate cannot move freely, tremendous pressures build up along this junction. The jumbled nature of the surface landscape is the manifestation of stress far below the surface of the earth, often as much as 200 or 300 miles deep. From time to time, this pressure becomes too great; the underlying rock breaks loose with dramatic and sometimes catastrophic results, and the land surface actually moves. This happened in the Olema Valley in 1906, and the result was the devastating San Francisco earthquake. At that

---

Bear Valley

Distance: 9 miles, nice family trail.

Terrain: Mainly level, a few small hills.

North Beach

Distance: 17 miles

Terrain: Hilly, one steep climb and descent to the Point Reyes Lighthouse.

Bicycle Rental: Available in the towns of Olema and Point Reyes Station.

Accommodations: Tourist services are available in nearby towns. Vehicle camping is not permitted in the park. There are, however, four hike-in campgrounds; Sky, Glen, Coast, and Wildcat. All campgrounds have restrooms and drinking water. Each campsite has a table, charcoal grill, and space for a tent. The park also has four picnic areas.

Access: Approach the seashore from the north or south on US 101 or California 1. From the east, take I-80 to California 37 to US 101. Major airports are located in Oakland and San Francisco.

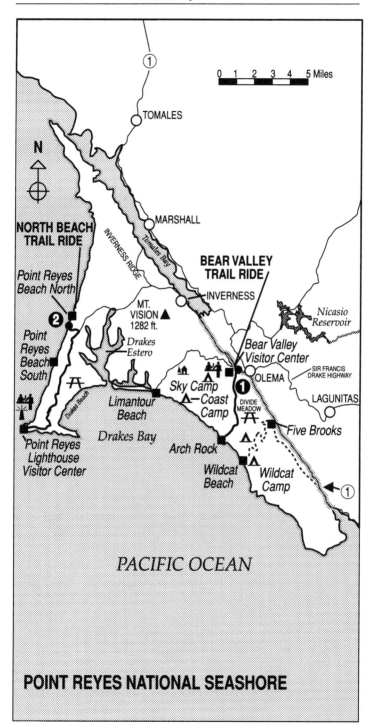

time, the Point Reyes Peninsula was thrust almost twenty feet northwestward.

For centuries before Europeans arrived, the Coast Miwok Indians inhabited these shores. Their lives were shaped by a pattern of changing seasons and the uneven temper of the weather along the coast. As peaceful hunters and gatherers, they moved about in this plentiful land to harvest acorns and berries, to catch salmon and shellfish, and to hunt deer and elk.

In the summer of 1579, these friendly Indians greeted Francis Drake, an English adventurer in the service of Queen Elizabeth I of England. Explorers from the outside world came and went in the years that followed. The English never returned to press their claim, but left it for the Spaniards to colonize. During the years of Spanish rule, the Miwok Indians of Point Reyes had been taken from their homelands to labor in Spanish missions. Except for a few Miwoks who had managed to evade the missionaries, and some survivors of the missions who wandered back after the Mexican revolution, Point Reyes had seen the last of its original inhabitants.

The first of two bicycle rides at Point Reyes National Seashore begins at the Bear Valley Visitor Center. Leaving the visitor center, take the Bear Valley Trail toward Arch Rock. Within the first quarter mile, I saw a half dozen deer grazing just off the trail. Beautiful golden grass-covered hills populated with dark green deciduous trees and coniferous pines make for a picturesque scene. The early morning air is incredibly fresh as the first of the sun's rays gleam against the trees and grasses.

As you ride along this rather smooth dirt and gravel trail, you can see many ferns on either side as the trail winds through thick forest for about two miles. A small creek runs noisely alongside your path. After a short uphill, the trail rolls downhill through a small hillside meadow. A type of green moss hangs from some of the trees. Just before the 4- mile mark, the trail reaches another small meadow, and up over a small rise, straight ahead, is the Pacific Ocean. Just out to sea, the fog hangs over the water. Take the trail to Arch Rock to see the coastline and the endless waves washing against the beach. The only sounds are those of the surf and seabirds out on a nearby seastack. A freshwater creek empties into the ocean to the left, and you can see seabirds avoiding waves as they feed on the beach. The fresh salt air and beautiful clear sky make for such a tranquil and peaceful scene that it is difficult to pull oneself away. The round- trip distance of this excellent family ride is 9 miles. Be careful of low tree branches and soft gravel in places along the trail.

The second bicycle excursion begins at North Beach and heads south to the Point Reyes Lighthouse. As you leave the beach area, the beach extends in either direction as far as the eye can see. Often, a light fog is rolling in and partially blocking out the sun as you reach Sir Francis Drake Highway and turn south. The surrounding golden rolling hills, void of trees, are pastureland for dairy cows.

As the route moves uphill, there are nice views of the ocean and surf. On the day of my ride, thick fog rolled in, just about blocking out the sun. The ground visibility was fine though. As you approach the lighthouse, you pass right through a dairy farm and begin an extremely steep ascent to the Point. Fortunately, it is of short distance. At the top, you find yourself in another world. Fog shoots right up the cliffs and surrounding ridges and races across the road with frightening speed. Large evergreens near the road have been blown grotesquely out of shape by the hurricane-force winds that have been clocked at over 100 miles per hour. The fog at Point Reyes occurs mainly from April to October as warm air masses pass over the much colder waters. On my trip, the fog was so thick that I could only catch occasional ghostly glimpses of the lighthouse, even though it was just over a hundred yards away.

Leaving the lighthouse, enjoy an excellent downhill back to the dairy farms. On the way down, you can often see sea lions sunning themselves on the cliffs far below, but you will need binoculars to get a good look. The round-trip distance of this ride is 17 miles. Be ready for cool, damp, and foggy conditions even if it is sunny and warm near the Bear Valley Visitor Center.

Other activities include hiking the nearly 150 miles of trails that wind through the park. Hike-in campsites are located at various points along many of these trails. There are also several short nature trails near Bear Valley Visitor Center that allow for educational walks of shorter duration. Beach-combing is popular along the North and South beaches and the Limantour Beach. Swimming at Drakes Beach is safe but the water is cold. Near Drakes Estero, bird-watching is a popular activity. During the winter, whales can be observed off the coast migrating between the Bering Sea and Baja, California. Field seminars are offered year-round in such activities as photography, art, and the natural history of Point Reyes National Seashore.

28. California: Redwood National Park

Redwood National Park is located along the northern coast of California. Within its boundaries grow the tallest trees in the world. Many of them reach heights of over 300 feet; the tallest at 368 feet is located in the southern part of the park near the town of Orick.

Redwood trees develop the greatest reported volume of living matter per unit of land surface. The giant sequoia, cousin to the coast redwood, grows larger in diameter and bulk, but not as tall. Coast redwoods survive to be about 2,000 years old, perhaps half the age of giant sequoia, and average probably 500 to 700 years. The living tree has no known killing diseases, and the insects associated with it cause no significant damage. Fire is the

Morning sunlight burns through the fog to reach these redwoods along Bald Hills Road.

worst natural foe, but usually to young trees which lack the thick bark protection. As with most conifers, the redwood lacks a taproot, and its broad, shallow root system sometimes provides inadequate support for the massive trunk. Wind topples many mature trees.

In the age of dinosaurs, redwood species were dominant over much of the Northern Hemisphere, including what is now the Arctic. The climate was then humid and mild over a much larger region than today. Over millenia, climate change reduced redwood habitat.

The abundant moisture and moderate temperatures of coastal northern California and extreme southern Oregon allow the redwood to flourish. This ocean-moderated climate is very humid with average yearly rainfall measuring between 25 and 120 inches, but annual precipitation seems less important than the frequent summer fog.

Bald Hills Road

Distance: 14 miles

Terrain: Very steep climb to the Lady Bird Johnson Grove, then generally level.

Prairie Creek

Distance: 14 miles

Terrain: Level

Bicycle Rental: Available in Eureka and Arcata.

Accommodations: Tourist accommodations are located in various towns along US 101. Four campgrounds are located within Jedediah Smith Redwoods, Del Norte Coast Redwoods, and Prairie Creek Redwoods State Parks. Sites offer a table, grill, and cupboard. Hot showers, restrooms, and disposal station are also provided. Over ten picnic areas are located in various sections of the park.

Access: Approach the park from the north or south on US 101. From the east, take US 199 or California 299 to US 101 to the park. The closest major airport is located in Medford, Oregon.

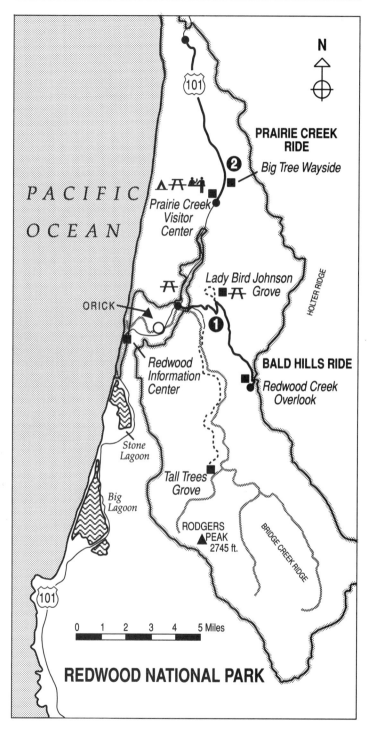

PRAIRIE CREEK
RIDE

Big Tree Wayside

2

PACIFIC

OCEAN

△ 🛧 👫⛺

Prairie Creek
Visitor
Center

Lady Bird Johnson
Grove

🛧

HOLTER RIDGE

ORICK

1

BALD HILLS RIDE

Redwood
Information
Center

Redwood Creek
Overlook

Stone
Lagoon

Big
Lagoon

Tall Trees
Grove

RODGERS
PEAK
2745 ft.

BRIDGE CREEK RIDGE

101

0 1 2 3 4 5 Miles

REDWOOD NATIONAL PARK

The passage of warm, moist marine air over the cold surface waters of the Pacific creates fog here almost daily in summer. It frequently lasts until afternoon, when it burns off. Another fog bank may move in before sunset. The fog decreases the trees' loss of water through evaporation and transpiration and adds moisture to the soil. The coast redwood is generally restricted to this coastal fog belt.

Almost from their discovery, coast redwoods inspired people to seek their preservation. Success first came in 1902 with the creation of Big Basin Redwoods State Park in a campaign led by the Sempervirens Club. National protection for redwoods was won in 1908, when President Theodore Roosevelt set aside Muir Woods National Monument under the Antiquities Act of 1906. Nearly ninety years of spirited advocacy finally bore fruit in 1968 when Congress created Redwood National Park.

The first bicycle ride begins from a small picnic area just off Bald Hills Road, in the south of Redwood National Park near the town of Orick. Proceeding through a small deciduous and fir forest, you soon arrive at Bald Hills Road. Turning east, you begin a steep, steady climb toward the great redwoods. Ferns can be seen along the road, and water drips to the ground from the condensation of fog near the treetops.

The route becomes even steeper as you near the 2-mile mark where, at the end of a bend in the road, tower the first giant redwoods, rising eerily through the thick fog. Continuing on, the road curves back and is steeper than ever. This particular climb was the steepest grade of any route I traveled in any of the national parks throughout the country. After about 2½ miles, the sun can be seen shining on the redwoods ahead. Just beyond and having made it through the fog, you will reach the Lady Bird Johnson Grove parking area. If you want to avoid this extremely difficult climb, you can drive up to the Lady Bird Johnson parking area and begin your bicycle ride from there. From the parking area, a self-guided nature trail leads the visitor on a 1-mile round-trip hike to the grove.

Sparkling sunlight shines on the huge trees as the road levels off and heads south underneath crystal-clear blue skies. At the 6-mile mark, you will come to a turnout on the right. From here, there is a spectacular view of the huge fog bank as it rolls in from the ocean and through the valleys below.

C-Line Road is the turnaround point. This is the road the shuttle buses take to the Tall Trees Grove, where the world's tallest tree at 368 feet grows. The round-trip distance of this bicycle ride is 14 miles. The return trip, mainly downhill, is very enjoyable.

The second ride begins at the Prairie Creek Visitor Center and heads north along Route 101. Try to begin your ride in the very early morning in order to avoid heavy afternoon traffic along the road. This is also a 14-mile round-trip ride, but this time over mainly level terrain. The route winds among thick stands of redwood. These huge trees grow right at the side of the road; often you can see how the road was built around them. There is a lot of shade along this route, but the sun does penetrate the thick redwood canopy in spots. The Big Tree Wayside is a good spot for a walk among these giants. The turnaround point of your ride is at the Coastal Drive turnoff. The route on the way back is generally a slight downhill.

Other activities at Redwood National Park include kayak trips on the Smith River in the northern part of the park, beachcombing and guided tidepool walks along the coastline, and fishing in many of the streams located throughout the

Coastal fog banks play an important role for the great redwoods. They reduce the trees' loss of water through evaporation and help keep the soil moist.

park. Hiking on the many self-guided nature trails as well as longer treks on trails such as the Coastal Trail or the Redwood Creek Trail are also very popular activities to enjoy year-round at Redwood National Park.

29. California: Sequoia National Park

Located on the western side of the Sierra Nevada, about fifty miles east of Fresno, is Sequoia National Park. Here, at elevations of between 4,000 and 8,000 feet, grow the largest trees on earth. The coast redwood may be the tallest, but the sequoia is unsurpassed for sheer massive bulk. The General Sherman Tree, recognized as the largest known sequoia, is so immense at its base that a dozen people with arms outstretched could not encircle the trunk.

The giant sequoia, much like the coast redwood, was once distributed over a large area of the world. However, a chang-

Even the giant sequoias don't live forever. But their wood takes a long time to decay.

ing climate, accompanied by the huge ice sheets of the last ice age, swept away all but the forests that remain on the western slopes of the Sierra Nevada.

Sequoia, the second oldest national park, was established in 1890 to preserve the remaining groves of giant sequoia trees so that future generations could behold their incredible size and beauty. As extensive as these groves appear to be, they do not begin to match the fine forest that once covered this area before the logging industry of the late 1800s nearly wiped it out.

Some of these giants reach ages of 4,000 years, largely due to their incredible bark. Its high tannin content protects it from insects, and its thickness of up to two feet makes it difficult for disease or fire to penetrate. In fact, fire is beneficial to these massive trees, in that by burning the fallen leaves and branches, the forest floor is cleared of debris, and seeds can more easily reach soil and germinate.

In the eastern part of the park is the high-country, an alpine environment where Mt. Whitney, the highest peak in the continental United States, rears its lofty summit to a height of 14,495 feet. Throughout this area, trails such as the High Sierra or John Muir trail lead the visitor through a true wilderness experience. The surrounding vegetation changes as rapidly as the elevation. At lower points, generally below 4,000 feet,

Giant Forest

Distance: 20 miles

Terrain: Fairly level, several gradually graded hills.

Bicycle Rental: Not available in or near the park.

Accommodations: Tourist services are available in the Grant Grove, Giant Forest, and Cedar Grove. Campgrounds are located at Sunset near Wilsonia within the Grant Grove, Lodgepole within the Giant Forest, Atwell Mill within Mineral King, as well as several other locations throughout the park. Picnic areas are located at Wolverton, Big Stump Basin, Columbine, Potwisha, and Hospital Rock.

Access: From the south, take California 99 to California 63 to California 198 to the park. From the north, take California 99 to California 180 to the park. The closest major airport is located in Fresno.

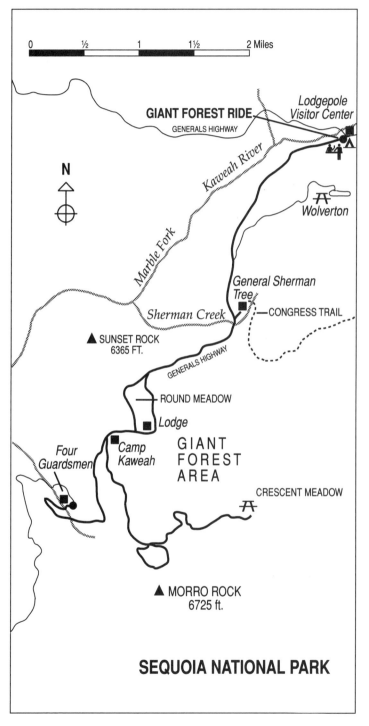

expect to see oak, cedar, and ponderosa pine. At higher points, lodgepole fir is common, and above 12,000 feet is a treeless alpine environment of knife-edged ridges as well as marshy meadows sprinkled with brightly colored wildflowers. Animals such as deer, black bear, coyote, mountain lion, and bobcat may be observed in various areas of Sequoia National Park.

This bicycle ride begins at the Lodgepole Visitor Center. Leaving the center, head south along the Generals Highway as it winds through beautiful pine and evergreen forest on its way to the Giant Forest several miles to the south. There is mountainside to the left of the route and valleys off to the right. Wind can be heard whistling through the tall trees, and above them the sky is crystal blue. A surprisingly large number of butterflies flutter through the evergreen-scented air, although there does not seem to be many wildflowers present.

As the road winds on, many areas of shade offer refuge from the afternoon sun. Ferns grow in these various shaded areas along the forest floor, and between the trees, distant pine ridges line the horizon. The road is a slight uphill as you approach the Wolverton turnoff, where a side road of a mile or so leads to a picnic area and horseback riding facilities. Continuing on, the road slopes downhill and soon reaches the General Sherman Tree, the largest living thing and one of the oldest. Its age is estimated to be about 2,500 years. There are many other large sequoia trees in this area; the Congress Nature Trail takes you among them. Regardless of whether there are many people in the area or not, there seems to be a hush of silence beneath these immense giants. The girth of these trees is astounding; pictures do not do them justice. One must stand at the base of a sequoia to really sense its awesome size.

Moving on, you can now see many sequoia alongside the road. At the Giant Forest, as many as eight sequoia can be counted within a diameter of about a hundred feet. The road winds around and between these gigantic trees that line both sides of the route. Once through the Giant Forest, an excellent downhill brings you to the Four Guardsmen, the turnaround point of this ride.

On the way back, a side excursion to Moro Rock enables you to enjoy magnificent views of the distant Sierra Nevada to the east and the silvery Kaweah River winding through a valley almost 4,000 feet straight down. Just beyond the Giant Forest, take the Round Meadow Road back to see many more large sequoia right alongside the road, including the Puzzle Corner Tree that fell on January 21, 1943, following a severe winter storm. Its age was estimated at 2,700 years. Green moss grows on most of the trees in this area, and in some spots along this road ferns grow so closely that they appear to form a carpet on the forest floor.

The round-trip distance of this bicycle ramble is 13 miles. Side excursions such as those mentioned would increase the distance to just over 20 miles. The best time to ride is the early morning when traffic is light, the temperatures are cooler, and wildlife is out feeding.

Other activities include walks along many of the nature trails that wind among the giant sequoia trees. Backcountry hikes along the High Sierra or John Muir trails offer a superb wilderness experience in a grand alpine setting. Horseback riding trips of two hours or several days lead from many points to the peace and serenity the backcountry offers. Fishing for trout is popular in many of the hundreds of streams

The General Sherman Tree is not only the largest living thing, it is probably also the most photographed.

and lakes located throughout the park. During the winter, downhill skiing is enjoyed at the Wolverton Ski Bowl, and cross-country skiing is also popular in various areas of Sequoia National Park.

30. California: Yosemite National Park

About 200 miles east of San Francisco, amidst the towering Sierra Nevada range, is one of the most beautiful valleys in the world, Yosemite. Sheer granite walls, domes, and spires rise many thousands of feet straight up from the flat valley floor. It is from these breathtaking precipices that half of America's highest waterfalls plunge to their destiny on the valley floor far below.

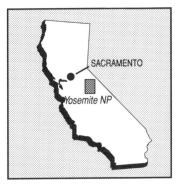

The most splendid of the valley's falls is Yosemite Falls, which drops just beyond the Three Brothers in two great leaps, a total of 2,425 feet, the height of over thirteen Niagaras stacked up on top of each other. Bridalveil, Illilouette, Nevada, and Vernal are all much loftier than Niagara, and the highest single plunge of them all is Ribbon Falls which spills an incredible 1,612 sheer feet. Nowhere else in the country is there so striking a collection of waterfalls in so small an area.

Yosemite Valley is probably the world's best example of a glacier-carved canyon. Its leaping waterfalls, towering cliffs, rounded domes, and massive monoliths make it a preeminent natural marvel. These attributes have inspired poets, painters, photographers, and millions of visitors beginning with John Muir for more than a hundred years. Nowhere else in the park is the sense of scale so dramatic.

Yosemite Valley is characterized by sheer walls and a flat floor. Its evolution began when alpine glaciers lumbered through the canyon of the Merced River. The ice carved through weaker sections of granite, plucking and scouring rock but leaving harder, more solid portions such as El Capitan and Cathedral Rocks intact. The ice also greatly enlarged the canyon that the Merced River had carved through successive uplifts of the Sierra. Finally, the glacier began to melt and the terminal moraine left by the last glacial advance into the valley dammed the melting water to form ancient Lake Yosemite, which sat in the newly carved U-shaped valley. Sediment eventually filled in the lake, forming the flat valley floor you see today. This same process is now filling Mirror Lake at the base of Half Dome.

The valley is a mosaic of open meadows sprinkled with wildflowers and flowering shrubs, oak woodlands, and mixed conifer forests of ponderosa pine, incense cedar and Douglas fir. Wildlife from monarch butterflies to mule deer and black bear flourishes in these communities. Around the valley perimeter, waterfalls crash to the floor. During May and June they reach their maximum flow, while in September and October they slow to a bare trickle. Yosemite National Park is much more than just Yosemite Valley, for the valley comprises less than 1 percent of the park's land area. The high-country has some of the most rugged, sublime scenery in the Sierra. In summer the meadows, lakes, and exposed granite slopes teem with life. Due to the short growing season, the plants and animals take maximum advantage of the warm days to grow, bloom, and store food for the long, cold winter ahead.

Tuolumne Meadows at 8,600 feet is the highest sub-alpine meadow in the Sierra. In the summer, Tuolumne Meadows is a favorite starting point for backpacking trips and day hikes. The meadows are spectacular in early summer, abounding in wildflowers and wildlife.

Giant sequoia groves can be found in several locations throughout the park. The most famous of these groves is the Mariposa Grove located in the southernmost part of the park.

As you view these trees, keep in mind that they have been here since the beginning of history in the Western world. The Mariposa Grove's grizzly giant is 2,700 years old and is thought to be the oldest of all sequoia.

The bicycle ride in Yosemite National Park begins at the Yosemite Valley Visitor Center. Heading west on a section of the 8 miles of paved bike paths in the park, you will find yourself enveloped in a beautiful mixed conifer forest of pine, cedar, and fir. As you might expect, generous shade is offered along the path by these 100- to 200-foot giants. In turn, these mighty trees are dwarfed by the canyon walls and cliff-faces that reach several thousand feet into the sky.

After about one mile you will arrive at one of the highest waterfalls in the world, Yosemite Falls. In two great leaps, the Yosemite Creek plunges from the towering cliffs and into the valley to join the Merced River. The first drop is just over 1,400 feet, while the second is around 1,000 feet, creating a very picturesque scene that is enhanced by a border of tall conifers along a quarter-mile walkway leading up to this most magnificent waterfall. The waterfall is at its best in the spring, when

The Merced River flows through a mixed forest of conifers and deciduous trees, with El Capitan in the background.

it thunders from the winter runoff. In the autumn, it very often is dry.

Past the falls area, join the one-way park road that will lead you into the lower end of the valley and El Capitan. The park road negotiates itself through the thick conifer forest creating a corridor as it goes. The smell of pine in the morning air is strong, and it is about here that you may realize that from a bike, this incredible valley seems much less congested than it does from behind the wheel of a car. You are able to stop just about anywhere along the park road, unlike the motorist, and thus will be able to experience the many spectacular sights more fully than your counterpart.

The Merced River begins to flank this route several miles into the ride. It is a very peaceful river during the summer and provides many opportunities for outstanding photographs, if the photographer is adventurous enough to leave the park road and experience the river close up as it winds through pine forest and wildflower meadows. Towering canyon walls provide a backdrop for many of these pictures.

Soon you arrive at El Capitan. Larger than the Rock of Gibraltar, at 3,600 feet it is said to be the largest single block of granite in the world. Its sheer cliff challenges rock climbers

---

Yosemite Valley

Distance: 17 miles, bike trails are nice for family rides.

Terrain: Level

Bicycle Rental: Available within the park at Curry Village and Yosemity Village.

Accommodations: Restaurants, stores, and lodging are available in Yosemite Valley and at Wawona, El Portal, Tuolumne Meadows and White Wolf. Campgrounds are situated throughout the park. One in the valley and others at Wawona and Hodgdon Meadow are open all year. No utility hookups are available, but all campgrounds have restrooms. Picnic areas are found throughout the park.

Access: From the south, take California 99 to California 41 to the park. From the west, take California 120 to the park. From the east, take US 395 to California 120 to the park. The closest major airports are located in Reno and Sacramento.

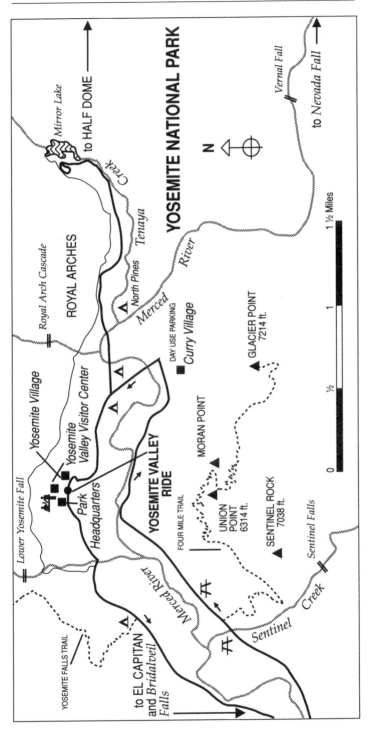

that come from all around the world. On this day, its granite outline was enhanced by the crystal-clear blue skies.

Take the second turnoff back to Yosemite Village at about the 6-mile mark. Just after connecting with the one-way park road that leads into the valley along its southern end, there are excellent views of Bridalveil Falls (620 feet) and El Capitan across the valley to the north. Huge boulders, many the size of a small house, can be seen scattered about the canyon floor. Ferns are occasionally seen in this area because of less direct sunlight caused by the high southern canyon walls. Rock spires, domes, and pinnacles can be viewed to the south of the route, while across the valley to the north, Yosemite Falls can again be observed this time from farther range.

Soon you are back in the village area. Take the bike trail that leads toward the visitor center and then east just past the campgrounds. This trail takes you past the Royal Arches and offers views of Glacier Point to the south. Tenaya Creek meanders alongside and soon leads to Mirror Lake. Across this small lake you will be treated to point-blank views of Half Dome, one of Yosemite's most famous landmarks. From here, your return ride to the visitor center completes this 17-mile jaunt through one of the most picturesque valleys in the world. Allow at least a half day for photos, stops, and wandering. The bike trails are excellent for family rides, but the park roads should be used by only experienced adult cyclists. The long-distance rider may find the route to Glacier Point or the Tioga Road a greater and more satisfying challenge.

Other activities include hiking the short trails that lead to many of the highest waterfalls in the country. Camping and, of course, campfire talks are popular family activities during the summer. Children 8 to 12 years of age can participate in the Junior Rangers Program, while adults can participate in field seminars on such subjects as photography, backpacking, and geology. In the backcountry, backpacking, mule, and horseback trips of several days or weeks are especially popular during the summer months. Overnight camps are set about ten miles apart and offer showers and meals served family style.

During the winter months, cross-country skiers can choose from more than 50 miles of trails, while the slopes at Badger Pass challenge the downhill skier. A large outdoor skating rink is located near Curry Village. As you can see, summer or winter, a diversity of enjoyable activities awaits the visitor to one of this country's most beautiful national parks, Yosemite.

PART VI

31. Introduction to the Northwestern Parks

The parks of the northwest include Crater Lake National Park in Oregon, Glacier National Park in Montana, Mt. Rainier National Park, Mt. St. Helens National Volcanic Monument, and Olympic National Park in Washington.

Crater Lake is located in the Cascade range of southern Oregon. Its incredible blue waters are known world-wide as a scenic wonder. The bicycle ride around the lake leads you past Wizard Island, a volcanic cone rising above the surface of the lake on its western end. To the north of the lake lies the Pumice Desert, where volcanic ash reaches a depth of 50 feet. A little farther along you will reach Cleetwood Cove, where tour boats take visitors for a tour of Crater Lake including a stopoff

McDonald Falls in Glacier National Park.

at Wizard Island. The Pinnacles can be visited in the southeastern part of the park in an area away from the lake.

Glacier National Park was named for the ancient massive ice sheets that carved the mountains into the horns and knife-edged ridges seen today. On your bicycle excursion through Glacier you will pass many waterfalls that send streams of water cascading from hanging valleys. You will also pass through wildflower prairies and pine-scented forests on your way to Logan Pass. Additional main attractions of Glacier National Park include St. Mary Lake in the eastern part of the park and Lake McDonald in the west, both having water bluer than you can imagine. Triple Divide Peak sends snowfall and rainfall to three different oceans depending upon which side of the mountain it lands. The Garden Wall and McDonald falls are located along the main park road and each in their own way is quite scenic.

Mt. Rainier is known as "The Mountain" to the people of Seattle and Tacoma, for it dominates their skyline on a clear day. Mt. Rainier, at 14,410 feet the highest peak in the Cascades, is actually a volcano capable of reawakening in the future. Your bicycle ride at Mt. Rainier will take you to such scenic features as Christine, Comet, and Narada falls, while also passing the Nisqually Glacier that has been advancing since the 1940s. From Paradise you can take a hike to the ice caves before returning down the mountain in an excellent coast almost all the way to Longmire. Sunrise, located on Mt. Rainier's northeastern flank, is also a good area to cycle, with spectacular views of the mountain as well as its glaciers.

Mt. St. Helens is the most recent example of volcanic activity in the forty-eight contiguous states. After 123 quiet years, Mt. St. Helens reawakened in the spring of 1980. The lateral blast toppled 230 square miles of forest north of the mountain. The bicycle ride into the monument takes you through this devastated area, a place where huge trees lie on their sides, blown down like matchsticks from the incredible blast. Everywhere ash and pumice cover the ground in this strange gray landscape. Spirit Lake can be seen from Cedar Creek, Donny Brook, and Windy Ridge, while the best views of the lava dome and crater of Mt. St. Helens is from Windy Ridge.

Olympic National Park is located on the Olympic Peninsula in the state of Washington. It is a wonderfully diverse land of fog-shrouded beaches, glacier-clad high mountain peaks, and a temperate rain forest in between. The bicycle rides will lead you through the Hoh rain forest where huge red cedar,

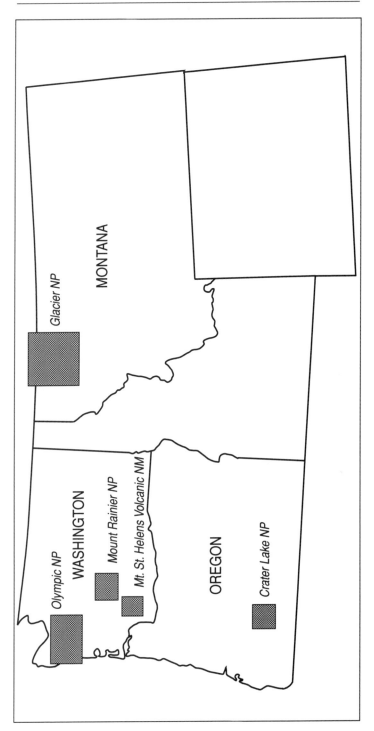

Sitka spruce, Douglas fir and Western hemlock grow in abundance, as well as to Hurricane Ridge, where after a several-hour ascent you can experience spectacular views of Mt. Olympus and the Olympic mountains to the south. Additional areas to visit include the Pacific coast near Rialto Beach, Sol Duc Hot Springs, the Queets rain forest and Lake Crescent, to name a few.

32. Oregon: Crater Lake National Park

Located in the rolling mountains and evergreen forests of the Cascade range in southern Oregon, about sixty miles north of Klamath Falls, is Crater Lake National Park. Upon first sight, it does not take the first-time visitor long to see why this lake is recognized worldwide as a scenic wonder. The color of Crater Lake is remarkable, for its brilliance is like that of a shining blue sapphire. The intensity of color is just incredible.

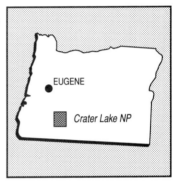

Why so blue? Crater Lake is very clear, because its water is as pure as distilled water. Sunlight gets absorbed color by color as it passes through the clear water. First the reds go, then orange, yellow, and green. Last to be absorbed are the blues. Only the deepest blue gets refracted back to the surface, from

Mt. Thielsen in the background, seen from Hillman Peak, across the Pumice Desert, where ash lies 50 ft. deep.

as deep as 300 feet, the natural limit of penetration. The water is, of course, no more blue than the sky is blue.

The plateau base of the Cascades was built as the earth's crust folded and uplifted, pushing seas westward. Molten rock pushed forcefully toward the surface, creating both violent eruptions and the welling up of lava through enormous cracks. In recent geologic time, the past 750,000 years, explosive eruptions built a string of volcanos on this extensive plateau base. This Cascade range of volcanoes extends from Canada's Mt. Garibaldi to Lassen Peak in northern California. One of these great volcanoes, Mt. Mazama, now holds Crater Lake.

For half a million years this mighty volcano produced massive eruptions interrupting long periods of quiet. Ash, cinders, and pumice exploded upward, building the mountain to a height of about 12,000 feet. Parasitic cones on Mazama's flanks created today's Scott and Hillman peaks. About 6,840 years ago, the climactic eruptions occurred. Ash from these eruptions lies scattered over eight states and three Canadian provinces. Approximately 5,000 square miles were covered with a blanket of ash at least six inches thick. In the park's Pumice Desert, ash lies 50 feet deep. Incredibly, the explosions of Mt. Mazama were forty times greater than those of Mt. St. Helens in 1980. The magma chamber was emptied and the volcano collapsed, leaving a huge bowl-shaped caldera in its place. The high mountain was gone. At first the caldera floor was too hot to hold water. Renewed volcanism sealed the caldera and built the Wizard Island and Merriam cones, volcanoes within a volcano.

As volcanic activity subsided, water began to collect. For the past 1,000 years the volcano has not stirred. Springs, snow, and rain began to fill the caldera. As the lake deepened and widened, evaporation and seepage balanced the incoming flow. The depth now varies less than a meter annually in this, the nation's deepest lake at 1,932 feet.

These fiery avalanches sometimes interruped the lives of Native Americans near Mt. Mazama. The Indians interpreted Mazama's violent eruptions before its collapse as a war between two gods, Llao and Skell. Shamans forbade most Indians to view the lake, and the Indians offered no information about the lake to pioneers who criss-crossed the area for fifty years without discovering it. In 1853, while searching for the Lost Cabin Gold Mine, a small party of prospectors, including John Wesley Hillman, accidentally "discovered" Crater Lake.

The bicycle ride at Crater Lake National Park begins at the Rim Village Visitor Center. As you leave the visitor center and head in a clockwise direction along the Rim Drive toward North Junction, the views of Crater Lake are just fantastic. The water is very calm and its color a fabulous deep blue. About two miles into the ride you will come to Discovery Point where a party of prospectors first saw the lake in 1853. Directly ahead is Wizard Island, a small volcanic cone produced by seething fire within the caldera after the destruction of Mt. Mazama. To the left of the route are beautiful mountain views.

Near the turnouts what look to be chipmunks are actually golden-mantled ground squirrels. They are quick to grab a handout if offered. Pinyon pine and shasta red fir trees are prevalent as your route turns temporarily away from the lake and up and around the Watchman. The Watchman, 8,025 feet, is a high rim peak from which the lake was sounded at 168 positions by lookouts in 1886. The peak was later named for this function.

Snow can be seen in many places near Hillman Peak even though it is an early August day. The Cascade range forces

The waters of Crater Lake are as deep as its rim walls are high—an amazing 1,972 ft. at its deepest point.

moisture-laden Pacific winds to rise and drop heavy precipitation. Wind, water, and ice continue to sculpt the landscape, and snow usually blankets Crater Lake National Park from October to July. Snowfall provides most of the park's annual 69 inches of precipitation. The average fall is 50 feet—yes, feet—per year.

This route is generally uphill for about the first five miles, but then after leaving a turnout that provides magnificent views of Mt. Thielsen and the Pumice Desert, the road is downhill to the North Junction.

Heading east past North Junction after a short half-mile uphill, the Rim Drive winds downhill around Llao Rock and through a thick, cool forest of spruce, fir, and pine trees on its way to Cleetwood Trail and the tour boat landing. Two- hour boat tours take visitors for closeup views of the Phantom Ship, and drop off passengers on Wizard Island for a leisurely stroll if desired. Several picnic areas can also be found along the northern rim with beautiful scenic views of the lake.

The Rim Drive is mainly uphill from the tour boat area to the Cloudcap turnoff. A nice downhill then leads you to Castle Rock. It is from a turnout in this area that you will get your first views of the Phantom Ship a couple of miles in the

---

Rim Drive

Distance: 33 miles

Terrain: Hilly, one steep descent near Vidae Falls and one steep climb just past the park headquarters.

Bicycle Rental: Available in the towns of Medford and Ashland.

Accommodations: The rustic Crater Lake Lodge, with dining room, is open at Rim Village from mid-June to early September. Snacks, meals, gifts, and film are sold daily at the Coffee Shop. A camper store sells groceries and limited supplies from June through September. Campgrounds are located at Mazama and Lost Creek. Picnic areas are found at various points along the Rim Drive.

Access: From the north, take I-5 to Oregon 138 to the park. From the south, take I-5 to Medford, take Oregon 62 north to the park. The closest major airports are located in Medford and Eugene.

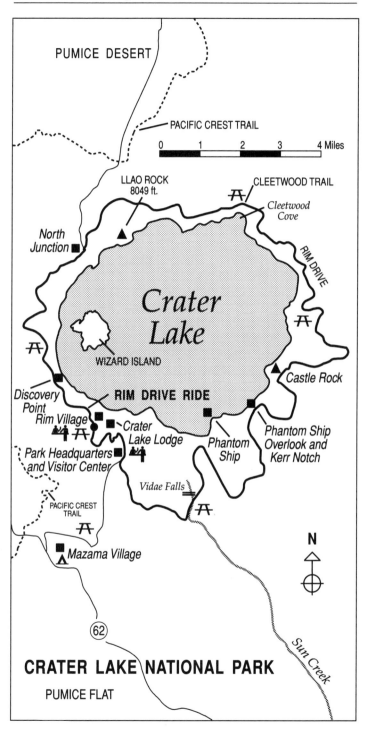

PUMICE DESERT

PACIFIC CREST TRAIL

0   1   2   3   4 Miles

LLAO ROCK
8049 ft.

CLEETWOOD TRAIL

Cleetwood
Cove

North
Junction

RIM DRIVE

*Crater
Lake*

WIZARD ISLAND

Castle Rock

RIM DRIVE RIDE

Discovery
Point
Rim Village

Crater
Lake Lodge

Phantom
Ship

Phantom Ship
Overlook and
Kerr Notch

Park Headquarters
and Visitor Center

Vidae Falls

PACIFIC CREST
TRAIL

N

Mazama Village

62

CRATER LAKE NATIONAL PARK

PUMICE FLAT

Sun Creek

distance. Turning briefly inland, your route continues downhill to the Pinnacles turnoff. The Pinnacles are volcanic spires and columns that solidified around gas and steam vents. They are located about six miles to the southeast of the Rim Drive.

Back on the Rim Drive, Kerr Notch provides very good views of the Phantom Ship through the trees about one mile away. Turning again inland, your route climbs steadily for about two miles before culminating in a great downhill that leads to Vidae Falls. Continuing on, this route winds through a heavily forested section of the park on its way to the park headquarters. It was in this area that I most thought about the animals that can be seen in Crater Lake National Park. Although I did not see any this day, elk, fox, deer, porcupine, and black bear are present.

From the park headquarters, the Rim Drive climbs steeply on this last leg of the ride. The total distance of this ride is 33 miles. Allow at least four hours to all day if you choose to take a boat tour, hike a trail, or picnic in one of the many picnic areas. Other activities at Crater Lake include hiking the many nature trails that lead to various points of interest in the park. Backcountry hiking along a section of the Pacific Crest Trail can be a very enjoyable and satisfying experience. Narrated boat tours leave from Cleetwood Cove taking visitors for a tour of the lake and a stop at Wizard Island. Ranger-led hikes and campfire talks during summer months are a special treat for children. During the winter, which lasts for eight months, cross-country skiing and snowmobiling are very popular activities at Crater Lake National Park.

33. Montana: Glacier National Park

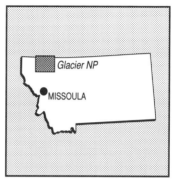

Located in the northwest of the state of Montana, amidst the Rocky Mountains thirty miles east of Kalispell, is Glacier National Park. This is a land of high-mountain adventure, a land that sets the senses soaring. Here you will find lofty mountain ranges with sculptured glacial valleys, ice-cold lakes that mirror mountains and sky, wildflowers and wildlife flourishing in alpine meadows, and prairie grasslands. Glacier National Park was named not for the glaciers that exist today, but for the ancient massive ice sheets that during the last million years carved the valleys and peaks and dug the lake beds, then finally melted away about 10,000 years ago.

The mountains visible today originated as sediments deposited in an ancient sea more than a billion years ago. For

The Going-to-the-Sun Highway follows the northern shore of St. Mary Lake .

millions of years, this bottom ooze slowly hardened into thick layers of limestone, mudstone, and more recently, sandstone rock. Then, about 65 million years ago, tensions building up within the earth's crust became so massive that these rocks began to warp and fold and finally break. A huge slab of rock slid from the west, up and over the eastern ranges. The pressures continued for millions of years, until eventually a 300-mile-long section of the earth's crust had been thrust 40 miles to the east. In its path, it covered rock a billion years younger in age. In other parts of the world, this process has also created mountain systems, but few can rival the Lewis Overthrust of Glacier National Park.

More recently, this rugged landscape has been carved by glaciers. These bodies of ice cut U-shaped valleys with tributary hanging valleys from which streams plunge to the main valley floor. In the upper elevations the glaciers are still at work.

Just to the north of Glacier National Park, across the international border in Alberta, Canada, is Waterton Lakes National Park. These parks, at the urging of many people, have been united as Waterton/Glacier International Peace Park. This land of natural splendors is dedicated to peace, one of humanity's highest goals, and to an international friendship that has few rivals.

Though administered by separate countries and divided by the international boundary, the parks are at the same time united in the most natural of ways. Glaciers carved the Upper Waterton Valley which lies in both nations, the native plants and animals are similar, and the massive Rocky Mountains span the two countries. Long before European explorers and settlers began to venture into the Rockies, the peoples native to this region shared the bounties of the land and considered it one.

In the mid 1700s things began to change. The quest for furs drew trappers deep into these mountains, and artificial limits were drawn marking the domains of the great fur-trading companies of the west. Then, in 1818, the 49th parallel to the Continental Divide was established as the international boundary between the territory of the United States and what was then territory owned by Great Britain, arbitrarily dividing the natural land area of today's Waterton/Glacier.

In the late 1800s, farsighted men such as Kootenai Brown in Canada and George Bird Grinnell in the United States labored to persuade their governments to set aside parts of the Rockies as wilderness recreational havens to be preserved for future generations. Their goals were reached in 1895 when Waterton Lakes National Park was established and in 1910 when Glacier was created. As the years went by, people in both nations recognized the natural unity of the parks, and largely through the efforts of Rotary International of Alberta and Montana, the United States Congress and the Canadian Parliament in 1932 established the first international peace park in the world: Waterton/Glacier International Peace Park. The park symbolizes the bonds of peace and friendship between the people of the United States and Canada.

The bicycle adventure at Glacier National Park begins from the St. Mary Visitor Center at the very eastern end of the park. Here the wildflower prairies of western Montana give way to the mighty horns and knife-edged ridges of the Rocky Mountains. As you head briefly north before turning west onto the famous Going-to-the-Sun-Highway, the morning silence is broken by hundreds of birds calling and singing their melodies from the nearby trees. Soon you cross the sparkling clear St. Mary River that drains from the dazzlingly beautiful

The McDonald River runs through a mixed conifer forest just east of Lake McDonald.

St. Mary Lake. The river will head northeast through Canada and empty into the Hudson Bay.

Turning west along the northern shore of St. Mary Lake, a sea of peaks retreat in the distance to the west. The early morning sun against these mountains and ridges is an incredible sight. This is definitely one of the most beautifully scenic parks in the country. Absolutely breathtaking. It is very easy to see why the French explorer Pierre La Verendrye called this 'the land of shining mountains.'

The waters of St. Mary Lake are very clear, and the rhythmic rustling of waves against the shoreline is quite relaxing. Countless purple wildflowers line the road as it heads toward Logan Pass. The trees in this part of the park are mostly deciduous, but there are a few pine and spruce.

From Two Dog Flats there is an excellent view across wildflower meadows of East Flattop Mountain to the north, and to the south the glistening surface of St. Mary Lake catches your eye. Many tiny rivulets empty into the lake, periodically breaking the silence of the early morning. The only other sounds are those of birds, crickets in the grass, and the wind.

After about five miles, there is a parking turnout with a superb view of Triple Divide Peak, whose waters flow to three

---

Going-to-the-Sun-Highway

Distance: 35 miles

Terrain: First several miles generally level, then a long sometimes steep ascent to Logan Pass. On the return trip you can coast all the way back to St. Mary Lake.

Bicycle Rental: Available in Apgar and Columbia Falls.

Accommodations: Tourist accommodations are located in surrounding villages as well as within the park at Apgar, Lake McDonald, Many Glacier, and Rising Sun. Campgrounds are found along the main park road and in the backcountry. Campgrounds along the main park road have fireplaces, tables, restrooms, and cold running water, utility connections are not provided. Campgrounds in the backcountry offer fireplaces, tables, and pit toilets.

Access: From the east, take US 2 to the park. From the south, take I-15 to US 2 to the park. From the west, take I-90 to US 93 to the park. The closest major airports are in Missoula, Helena, and Great Falls.

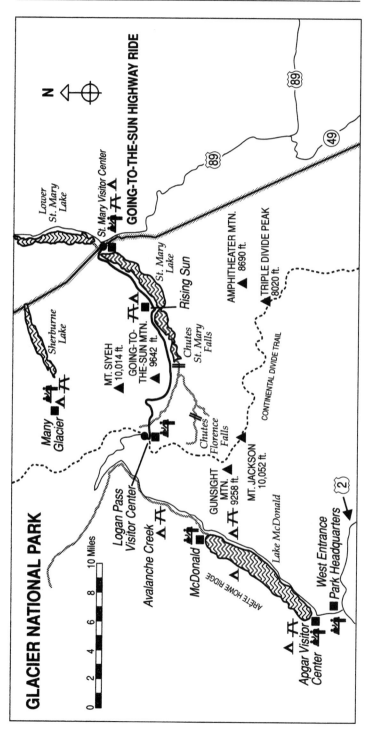

GOING-TO-THE-SUN HIGHWAY RIDE

GLACIER NATIONAL PARK

N

Lower St. Mary Lake

St. Mary Visitor Center

St. Mary Lake

Rising Sun

Sherburne Lake

AMPHITHEATER MTN. 8690 ft.

TRIPLE DIVIDE PEAK 8020 ft.

MT. SIYEH 10,014 ft.

GOING-TO-THE-SUN MTN. 9642 ft.

Chutes St. Mary Falls

CONTINENTAL DIVIDE TRAIL

Many Glacier

Chutes Florence Falls

GUNSIGHT MTN. 9258 ft.

MT. JACKSON 10,052 ft.

Logan Pass Visitor Center

Avalanche Creek

McDonald

Lake McDonald

ARETE HOWE RIDGE

West Entrance Park Headquarters

Apgar Visitor Center

10 Miles

0 2 4 6 8

oceans: the Pacific by the Columbia River, the Arctic by Hudson Bay, and the Gulf of Mexico via the Mississippi system.

Just past Rising Sun, the mountains you had been seeing all along close in rapidly as you begin the ascent to Logan Pass. The smell of pine and spruce from the surrounding coniferous forest is strong and reminds me of Christmas. Many of the spruce trees are perfectly symmetrical. At times the mountains seem to almost hang over the road as it winds through the thick forest.

At about the 13-mile mark there is a good view of the Jackson Glacier on the 10,052-foot Mt. Jackson just five miles to the southwest. The climb is getting steeper as you negotiate out of the thick coniferous forest and onto the more barren high mountain ridges. Just before leaving the forest, fireweed and yellow daisies are quite common along the road.

The last 3 miles to Logan Pass are a steep climb along mountain cliffs and ridges where many beautiful waterfalls tumble hundreds of feet down the mountainsides. In an alpine meadow to the left of the road are several pretty waterfalls that cascade between forests of spruce that look miniaturized far below. Just before reaching the Logan Pass Visitor Center you will pass through a tunnel. In several places over the last mile or so, water splashes down the cliffsides and onto or near the road, beckoning the hot cyclist into its mist.

From Logan Pass the high mountain scenery stretches in all directions. You can either continue on to Lake McDonald and the Apgar Visitor Center, or retrace your route as I did on this day. On the return trip down, you will be able to coast for a large part of the descent. Soon, you are back down in the fragrant meadows looking back at the picturesque mountain scenery. The round-trip distance of this ride is 35 miles. Allow at least half a day if not longer to enjoy this magnificent ride.

Other activities at Glacier National Park include hiking and camping, for more than 700 miles of trails criss-cross the park. Horseback riding trips are available at Apgar, Many Glacier, and Lake McDonald Lodge. Boating and fishing are quite popular on many of Glacier's lakes and streams. Ranger-guided walks and evening campfire programs are offered from late June through August. During winter, which lasts from October to April, cross-country skiing as well as snowshoeing is enjoyed by many of the visitors that come to experience the tranquility of the spectacular Glacier National Park.

34. Washington: Mount Rainier National Park

Located about fifty miles southeast of Seattle stands the highest peak in the Cascade range, Mt. Rainier at 14,410 feet. Nothing quite prepares visitors for their first view of it. There are a few higher peaks in the United States, but none that so dominates the surrounding landscape by its incredible towering mass.

Mt. Rainier reaches into the upper atmosphere to disturb great tides of moist maritime air as they flow eastward from across the Pacific. The resulting encounter creates spectacular cloud halos, wrings out the air, and produces a prodigious amount of snowfall. Paradise, located at 5,400 feet on the mountain's south slope, commonly has enough snow to bury the three-story-high Paradise Inn right up to its roof. Snowfall is heaviest from Paradise up to about 9,500 feet. At that height

Mt. Rainier is actually a volcano, and like Mt. St. Helens to the south, is capable of reawakening any day in a fiery fury.

the mountain rears above the wet maritime air masses and the amount of snowfall decreases.

The abundant snow gives birth to Mt. Rainier's glacier system, the largest single mountain system in the lower forty-eight states, consisting of 35 square miles of ice in twenty-seven named glaciers. Much of the great spectacle that so awes park visitors is attributable to these glaciers. Because of them, the mountain appears higher and more varied than it other-wise would, and there are deep valleys separated by high craggy ridges or broad plateaus such as those found at places like Sunrise on the northeastern flank of the mountain. From these overlooks the view drops off into valley depths 1,600 feet below, then abruptly soars up the slopes of Mt. Rainier. The mountain's height is thus accentuated by the glacial valleys.

The glaciers provide constant reminders of their conti-nuing activity. On warm days, avalanches of ice, snow, and rock make the mountain extremely dangerous. At any time, huge masses of snow and ice may break loose. Mudflows, another hazard, may suddenly gush downslope when huge quantities of water, mud, and rock trapped under glaciers break loose. The Kautz Mudflow of 1947 is the best-known example. It was caused when a high crest of mud built up by

Paradise

Distance: 24 miles

Terrain: A long sometimes steep ascent to Paradise. The ride back to Longmire is generally a coast all the way.

Bicycle Rental: Available in Yakima.

Accommodations: Tourist services are available within the park at Longmire, Paradise, and Sunrise. Along the park road camping is available at Cougar Rock, Ohanapecosh, andSunshine Point. Campgrounds are also located in the backcountry at Mowich Lake, Ipsut Creek, and White River. Over ten picnic areas are located throughout the park.

Access: From the south, take I-5 to US 12 to Washington 7 to Washington 706 to the park. From Seattle and Tacom,a take Washington 7 to Washington 706 to the park. From the east, take I-90 or I-82 to US 12 to Washington 123 to the park. The closest major airports are located in Seattle and Tacoma.

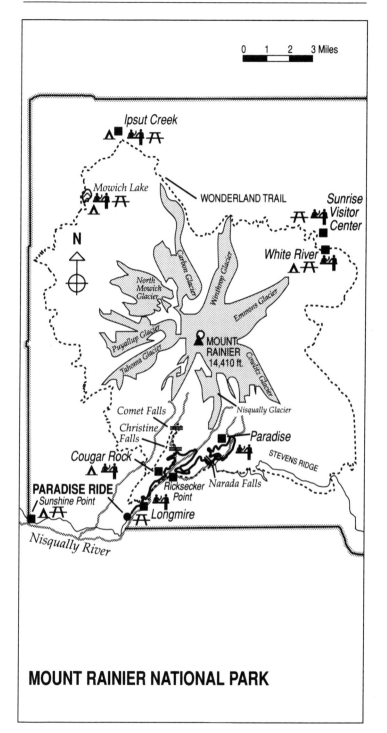

Ipsut Creek

Mowich Lake

WONDERLAND TRAIL

Sunrise Visitor Center

White River

N

Carbon Glacier

Winthrop Glacier

North Mowich Glacier

Emmons Glacier

Puyallup Glacier

Tahoma Glacier

MOUNT RAINIER
14,410 ft.

Cowlitz Glacier

Comet Falls

Nisqually Glacier

Christine Falls

Paradise

Cougar Rock

STEVENS RIDGE

PARADISE RIDE

Ricksecker Point

Narada Falls

Sunshine Point

Longmire

Nisqually River

MOUNT RAINIER NATIONAL PARK

197

heavy rain broke loose from behind a wall of ice and thundered down the slope, thrusting huge boulders before it, snapping trees like matchsticks and burying the park road under 50 feet of mud and debris.

Mt. Rainier as it is enjoyed today will not last long in terms of geologic time. The mountain is quite capable of re-awakening any day, perhaps in an eruption violent enough to return it to its dawning day. Mt. Rainier's identity as a volcano, if not immediately obvious from its size and shape, is betrayed by two craters on its summit. Evidence of the energy still ebbing within the craters is seen at caves along their rims, where steam has melted tunnels in the summit ice cap. It was steam vents such as these that saved the lives of Philemon Beecher Van Trump and Hazard Stevens who made the first documented climb to the summit in 1870.

The bicycle ride at Mt. Rainier National Park begins in the southwest of the park at Longmire and climbs 2,700 feet in elevation before reaching its destination at Paradise. Leaving Longmire, the park road winds uphill through a thick cedar, fir, and spruce forest. Most trees are at least 100 to 150 feet tall. Quite often ferns are seen alongside the road, and moss is common on the living trees as well as logs on the forest floor.

After just a half mile, a rushing stream can be heard but not yet seen in the forest. Around a curve in the road and there through the tall cedars is the Nisqually River, the source of the previously heard water. A short walk from the road down to the river gives you a close view of the power of water. Although the river is low this time of year (early August), from observing the riverbed of jumbled boulders you can perceive the awesome fury of the river during the spring when the stream is swollen from the winter's runoff.

At about the 1-mile mark, you will pass a small moss-and-lichen-covered cliffside just before reaching the tree bridges. The tree bridges are simply a pair of dead trees that allow passage to the far side of the Nisqually River.

The smell of campfires will fill the morning air as you approach the Cougar Rock Campground. Beyond at the 4-mile mark, the Comet Falls Trail leads the bike rider-turned-hiker 1.6 miles to the pretty 300-foot Comet Falls. Tall spruce and fir trees line the ridges at the top of the falls, while delicate and colorful wildflowers line the banks of the creek at the bottom. Other smaller falls can be seen along the hike.

Just ahead on this route, up steep roads, is Christine Falls. The falls drop about 50 feet to the left of the road and then an additional 20 to 30 feet underneath it. Continuing on, you will soon cross the Nisqually River Bridge, and as you head back to the south along a steep cliffside, a look back over your shoulder will reveal spectacular views of the Nisqually glacier and especially Mt. Rainier. To the right, in the valley far below, you can see the park road you were just on winding through the thick coniferous forest.

Take the turnoff to Ricksecker Point, where several overlooks provide dramatic views of the Nisqually River Canyon as well as the retreating mountains and ridges of the Cascades to the south and east. Looking back toward Mt. Rainier, you can see the Nisqually glacier that has been advancing since the 1940s.

At the 9-mile mark, the Narada Falls plummet 240 feet to the right of the road. This is the crystal-clear Paradise River on its way from the Paradise Valley to the Nisqually River. After several more twists in the road, you soon reach the Paradise Visitor Center where mountain, glacier, snowfield, and forest stretch in every direction as far as the eye can see.

The Paradise River rushes through the forest just above Narada Falls in the south of the park.

Even in July and August, snow lingers near Paradise. It's hard to imagine at this time of year that the three-story inn is almost buried by snow each winter. Nonetheless, just to the north along a snow field leading to the Ice Caves are breathtaking views of the great mountain.

The return ride back down to Longmire is pure enjoyment, for you can coast all the way except for about half a mile. The round-trip distance of this ride is 24 miles through very steep terrain. Allow at least a half day or a full day if taking one or more of the nature trails.

Other activities include hiking on the 300 miles of trails located throughout the park. The Wonderland Trail completely encircles the mountain, a distance of over 90 miles, with campsites located about every 10 miles. Many shorter nature trails lead to specific points of interest. Mountain climbing is also popular, with several thousand climbers making it to the summit each year. Fishing is allowed in all park waters, but some streams may be too cold to support much aquatic life. During the winter months, snowshoeing and cross-country skiing are very popular activities at Mt. Rainier National Park.

35. Washington: Mt. St. Helens National Volcanic Monument

In the Cascade range, less than a hundred miles south of Seattle and Tacoma, can be found the most recent example of volcanic activity in the forty-eight contiguous states. The 110,000-acre Mt. St. Helens National Volcanic Monument was created through congressional legislation in 1982 for research, education, and recreation for present and future generations.

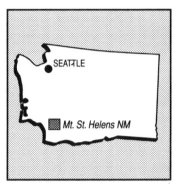

After 123 quiet years, Mt. St. Helens reawakened in the spring of 1980. Magma pushed up into the volcano, causing earthquakes and small ash emissions for six weeks, and a 300-foot bulge formed on the north side of the mountain.

The lateral blast leveled fully grown trees like toothpicks.

The May 18 eruption was triggered by an earthquake with a magnitude of 5.1 on the Richter scale. The swollen north flank slid into the Spirit Lake basin and down the North Fork Toutle River valley, forming the largest landslide in recorded history. Part of the avalanche surged into Spirit Lake, forming huge waves that sloshed 826 feet up the surrounding hillsides and swept thousands of trees and debris into the lake. A lateral blast produced a 650-degree-Fahrenheit rock-laden current of ash and hot gas traveling at hundreds of miles per hour. This blast toppled 230 square miles of forest north of Mt. St. Helens. A vertical column of ash erupted from the newly formed crater to a height of 15 miles. The ash, spreading eastward by prevailing winds, circled the earth in just two weeks.

Volcanic mudflows, dense mixtures of rocks and ash mixed with water and resembling wet concrete, flowed down all slopes of the volcano. Pyroclastic flows of fiery, broken rocks, 700-degree-Fahrenheit gas and ash came down the slopes at 60 miles per hour. These flows formed a pumice plain on the south shore of Spirit Lake.

When the ash cleared, Mt. St. Helens was 1,300 feet shorter. Spirit Lake was much larger, and the lush, green forest around it had been transformed into a blown-down, gray landscape. It was obvious that the powerful natural forces responsible for the

---

Bear Meadow

Distance: 23 miles

Terrain: Hilly, mainly uphill to Windy Ridge and downhill back to Bear Meadow.

Bicycle Rental: Available in Portland.

Accommodations: Accommodations are available in the nearby towns of Morton and Randle. Campgrounds are located at Saddle Dam, Merrill Lake, Cougar, Kalama Horse Camp, Swift, and Iron Creek. Picnic areas are found along Road 99 and during the summer snacks are available at a snack bar on Road 99 less than ten miles from the volcano.

Access: From the north or south, take I-5 to Washington 503 to Washington 90 then 25 and 99 into the monument. From the east, take US 12 to Washington 25 then 99 to the park. The closest major airports are located in Seattle and Tacoma.

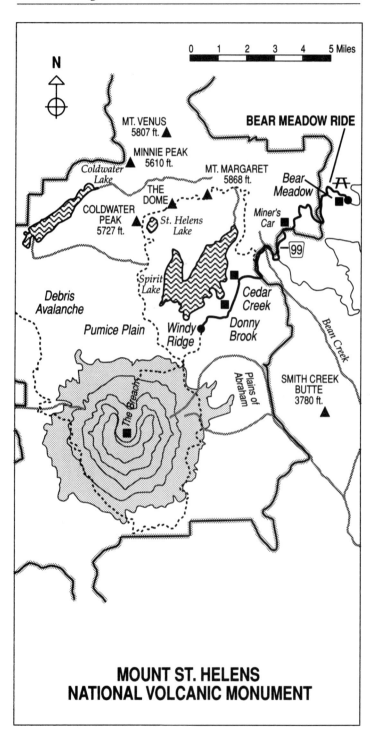

0 1 2 3 4 5 Miles

N

BEAR MEADOW RIDE

MT. VENUS
5807 ft. ▲

MINNIE PEAK
5610 ft. ▲

Coldwater Lake

MT. MARGARET
5868 ft. ▲

Bear Meadow

THE DOME ▲

Miner's Car

COLDWATER PEAK
5727 ft. ▲

St. Helens Lake

99

Spirit Lake

Cedar Creek

Bean Creek

Debris Avalanche

Pumice Plain

Windy Ridge

Donny Brook

SMITH CREEK BUTTE
3780 ft. ▲

The Breach

Plains of Abraham

MOUNT ST. HELENS
NATIONAL VOLCANIC MONUMENT

famed beauty of the Pacific Northwest were not just ancient history, but an ongoing natural process.

The bicycle adventure at Mt. St. Helens begins from the Bear Meadow parking area located on Highway 99 about fifteen miles northeast of the crater. Starting out, the first mile is downhill through a forest of mature spruce trees. These trees are still standing because they were protected from the blast by the mountain ridge to the west. After a short uphill and another downhill, you negotiate around a bend in the road, and there about ten miles away stands Mt. St. Helens. Steam rises from the immense lava dome that has built up over several years to form a cumulus cloud above the mountain.

Many small spruce trees, various bushes, and wildflowers can be seen returning to the devastated land in many places. Ash and pumice cover the ground, and huge uprooted trees litter the hillsides like matchsticks in every direction. Erosion is common on these hills due to the lack of vegetation since the eruption.

Continuing on, at about the 4-mile mark you will reach the miner's car. The miner was trapped in a mine several hundred

In the background, Mt. St. Helens, flanked in this view by two relics of the big blast.

yards away when the blast occurred. At the 6-mile mark, after negotiating a barren ridge there is a snack bar that serves barbecued chicken and ribs daily.

Stop alongside the road and listen for the pebbles and stones of ash that frequently roll down the hills and onto the road. The wind, which can be quite strong due to the elevation and lack of trees, is the source of this phenomenon. Also, since there are no trees there is next to no shade, making this a hotter ride than would normally be expected in this part of the country.

From Cedar Creek you will get your first views of Spirit Lake, its surface almost completely covered with dead trees. There are also good views of Spirit Lake farther up the route at both Donny Brook and at Windy Ridge, the turnaround point. From Windy Ridge the crater of Mt. St. Helens is just over four miles away, but this is the closest you can get. As one listens to the naturalist explain the events that took place in 1980, it is eerie to think that the distance just traveled by bike over a two- to three-hour period took the blast wave just one minute to travel.

The round-trip distance of this unique adventure is 23 miles. Allow about six hours or more to leisurely explore this volcanic monument.

Mt. St. Helens as she will look for the next few years: ashes, as far as the eye reaches.

Other activities include hiking the extensive trail system that allows spectacular views of every side of the volcano. Naturalist-led walks and talks from several points of interest within the monument are enjoyed by young and old alike. Mountain climbing to the summit of Mt. St. Helens is gaining in popularity. During the winter months, snowmobilers and cross-country skiers enjoy the Mt. St. Helens National Volcanic Monument blanketed in a shroud of pure white snow.

36. Washington: Olympic National Park

Located on the Olympic Peninsula in the extreme northwest corner of the state of Washington is Olympic National Park. It is a wonderfully diverse land of fog-shrouded beaches, glacier-clad mountain peaks, and in between the last thing one might expect to find, a temperate rain forest. Let's explore each of these worlds.

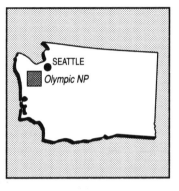

The coastal portion of Olympic National Park extends for about sixty miles along the Pacific Ocean. This coastline looks much as it did when early Indians built their first villages upon these shores, thousands of years before European explorers arrived. Huge sculptured arches and sea stacks as well as gigantic drift logs can be seen everywhere. The roar of crashing ocean surf drowns out the

Approaching Second Beach, near La Push on the Pacific Coast, a seastack is seen just off the shore.

sound of the gulls as they feed near the shoreline. The lucky visitor may witness one of the dramatic sunsets across the sheer vastness of the Pacific Ocean.

The Olympic Mountains rise almost from the ocean edge and intercept moisture-rich air masses that move in from the Pacific. As this air is forced over the mountains, it cools and releases moisture in the form of rain or snow. At lower elevations rain nurtures the forests, while at higher elevations snow adds to glacial masses that relentlessly carve the landscape. On Mt. Olympus, the highest of the peaks at about 8,000 feet, there are seven glaciers with ice roughly 1,000 feet thick in places. Over fifty glaciers can be found in the high-country as a whole. The mountains wring precipitation out of the air so effectively that areas on the northeast corner of the peninsula experience a rain shadow and get very little rain. The town of Sequim gets only 17 inches a year, while less than thirty miles away, Mt. Olympus receives some 200 inches falling mostly as snow.

In between the thundering surf at the coastline and the creaking of massive glaciers in the high mountains are the forests of Olympic. Temperate rain forests are rare. They can be found only in New Zealand, southern Chile, and here on the northwest coast of the United States in the valleys of the Quinault, Queets, and Hoh rivers. What defines a rain forest quite simply is rain, lots of it. On the Olympic coast precipitation averages 145 inches, more than 12 feet, every year.

The dominant species of trees in the rain forest are Western red cedar, Sitka spruce, Douglas fir, and Western hemlock. Several of these species grow to record sizes here in the Olympic rain forests. Nearly every bit of space is taken up with a living plant; lichens, mosses, ferns, and epiphytes cover just about everything, giving the rain forest its jungle-like appearance. This dense ground cover makes it difficult for seedlings to find available soil. Often seedlings fall on a decaying tree, which acts as a nurse log for the new trees. Eventually, the log rots completely away and young trees are left, up on stilt-like roots, all in a row.

The bicycle adventures at Olympic National Park will explore two of these worlds, the rain forest of the Hoh River and the high-country of Hurricane Ridge. Leaving the Hoh Visitor Center and heading west, the smell of morning campfires from a nearby campground fills the air. Huge ferns spot the forest floor and large quantities of moss drape the smallest to the largest trees. The Hoh River can be heard, though muffled by this thick forest undergrowth, rushing to the sea south of the route.

Many birds sing their songs from the huge Sitka spruce and Western red cedars. About a mile into this ride, the forest thickens and comes right up against the road. Even though brilliant sunlight illuminates the upper stories of the rain forest, little direct sunlight reaches the forest floor. Instead, the sunlight is reflected and refracted by the luxurious undergrowth, casting an amazing yellowish-green hue over the lower stories of the rain forest, and giving the Hoh Rain Forest the look of a prehistoric jungle.

The air temperature can feel chilly due to the dampness and the large amount of shade along the route, especially during the early morning hours and evening. Farther up the road you can see the Big Spruce Tree. At over 270 feet in height, it has a diameter of more than 12 feet and is approximately 500 to 550 years old. Many spruce with diameters near 10 feet may be observed throughout this area. Several turnouts provide scenic views of the Hoh River and the glacier-clad mountains beyond.

Even near the turnaround point of this ride, which is in the lower end of the forest at the entrance station, the moss is incredibly abundant and is as thick and thicker than shag carpet as it coats and drapes just about every tree in sight.

The beach is a wonderful place to walk—providing you know when the tides will occur.

The park road along this route is in good condition and generally level, except for one small hill. The round-trip distance of this unique ride is 11 miles.

The second bicycle ride at Olympic National Park begins from the Pioneer Memorial Visitor Center and heads for the high-country of Hurricane Ridge. As you might expect, the park road starts out uphill as it negotiates through a small deciduous forest that thickens as you ascend. After about two miles, the surrounding forest begins changing from deciduous to coniferous as the route swings back to the southeast and passes under a small bridge. Many patches of ferns can be seen along the road. The road curves back to the west and continues

---

Hoh Rain Forest

Distance: 11 miles

Terrain: Mainly level, except for one small hill.

Hurricane Ridge

Distance: 35 miles

Terrain: A long generally steep ascent to Hurricane Ridge. The ride back to the visitor center is generally a coast all the way.

Bicycle Rental: Available in Port Angeles.

Accommodations: Several motel units, cottages, cabins, and lodge rooms are available within the park at Kalaloch Lodge near Queets, at Log Cabin Resort and Lake Crescent Lodge along Lake Crescent, and Sol Duc Hot Springs Resort near Soleduck. The park has 18 campgrounds. Most consist of individual sites with tables and fireplaces. Piped water and toilet facilities are usually near a cluster of campsites. Gasoline and groceries are available at Fairholm General Store and Kalaloch Lodge. Picnic areas are found at Rialto Beach, Hoh Rain Forest, and Hurricane Ridge as well as several others.

Access: From the south, take I-5 to US 101 to the park. From the east, take I-90 to I-5 to Washington 16 to 3 to 104 to US 101 and into the park. The closest major airports are located in Seattle and Tacoma.

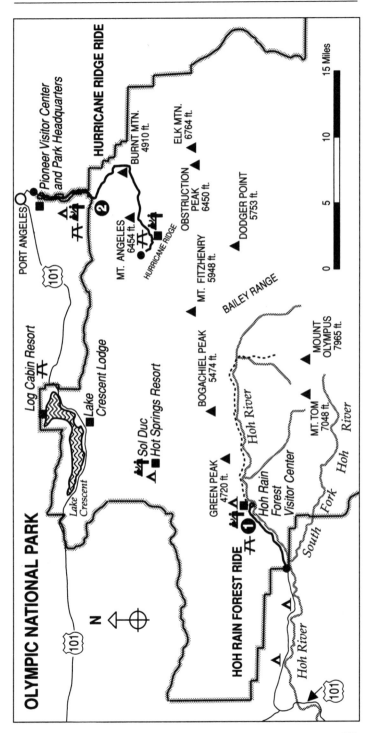

to climb at the 3-mile mark. Just past the 4-mile mark there is a magnificent view of the bay. A surprise downhill of about one mile brings you to the entrance station. Western hemlocks can be seen as you start uphill again. There are small violets and thousands of daisies in this area. Around the 8-mile mark there is an unbelievable view of valley, bay, and distant mountain peaks in the Cascades. At the next turnout you will be able to see Mt. Rainier toward the southeast almost 100 miles away.

Farther ahead you will pass through four separate tunnels, each at a length of around 100 to 200 yards. At the 10- mile mark, snow-capped ridges line the southern horizon. At 12 miles I saw a deer as the route relentlessly continued to climb. Moss can be seen on some of the trees in this area, but nothing like in the Hoh rain forest. The park road is still climbing at 14 miles, and again there are many yellow daisies.

The time of this ascent was during the late afternoon and early evening, so there was much shade along the road to keep me cool. During the morning or early afternoon, more sun would make for a warmer ride.

At 15 miles all sorts of wildflowers lined the road. Their mixture of color—reds, oranges, whites, dark blues, yellows, and violets—are gorgeous to the eye. At 16 miles this route still climbs as it offers good views to the east. Many small spruce trees with heights of about 10 to 30 feet populate this area.

At last, at the 17-mile mark you will reach Hurricane Ridge, where to the south you can see the glacier-clad mountains of the Bailey range, as well as Mt. Olympus. Many deer roam freely in these mountaintop meadows and quite often pass through the parking areas. Sometimes mountain goats can be spotted clinging to the steep cliffs above the park road.

Needless to say, Hurricane Ridge is the turnaround point of this ride. The descent is practically a coast all the way back to the entrance station, where after a short climb you can again coast to the visitor center. The round-trip distance of this alpine adventure is 35 miles.

The varied worlds of Olympic National Park can be enjoyed in other ways, including camping at over eighteen different established campgrounds. Horseback riding can take the visitor to places that roads simply cannot. Mountaineering and fishing are also quite popular. And hiking, whether it be a cross-park trek or along a shorter nature trail, is enjoyed by many a park visitor.

Bicycle Rental Addresses

Acadia:
In Bar Harbor and other nearby towns.

Cape Cod:
In the towns of Cape Cod.

Cape Hatteras:
On Ocracoke Island.

Great Smokies:
From the ranger station located near the entrance to Cades Cove.

Shenandoah:
In the towns of Front Royal and Waynesboro.

Big Bend:
In the town od Lajitas.

Gulf Islands:
From the campground store near Fort Pickens.

Padre Island:
In Corpus Christi.

White Sands:
In the town of Alamogordo.

Badlands:
In Rapid City and Custer.

Craters of the Moon:
In Sun Valley and Idaho Falls.

Grand Tetons:
At Moose, Jenny Lake, Signal Mountain, Colter Bay, and Jackson.

Rocky Mountains:
At Estes Park or Grand Lake.

Yellowstone:
In West Yellowstone and Colter Bay.

Bryce Canyon:
In the town of Rubys Inn just north of the park.

Grand Canyon:
In Flagstaff.

Petrified Forest:
In Pinetop- Lakeside, Springerville, and Flagstaff.

Saguaro:
In Tucson.

Zion:
In the town of Springdale located just south of the park.

Joshua Tree:
In Twentynine Palms.

Lassen:
From the campground store at Manzanita Lake.

Point Reyes:
In the towns of Olema and Point Reyes Station.

Redwood:
In Eureka and Arcata.

Sequoia:
Not available within or near the park.

Yosemite:
Within the park at Curry Village and Yosemite Village.

Crater Lake:
In the towns of Medford and Ashland.

Glacier:
In the towns of Apgar and Columbia Falls.

Mt. Rainier:
In Yakima.

Mt. St. Helens:
In Portland.

Olympic:
In Port Angeles.

BIBLIOGRAPHY

I. Books about the National Parks

National Park Guide, by Michael Frome. Chicago: Rand McNally, 1991.

National Parks of the West, by the editors of Sunset Books and Sunset Magazine. Menlo Park, CA: Lane Publishing Co., 1985.

National Parks: the family guide, by Dave Robertson. Pt. Roberts. WA: On Site!, 1991.

Reader's Digest: Scenic Wonders of America, by the Reader's Digest. Pleasantville, NY: The Reader's Digest Association, 1973.

National Geographic's Guide to the National Parks of the United States, by the National Geographic Society. Washington, D.C.: National Geographic Society, 1989.

National Parks of the U.S.A., by James V. Murfin. New York: Mayflower Books, 1980.

101 Wonders of America, by the editors of Country Beautiful. Waukesha, WI: Country Beautiful Corporation, 1973.

Reader's Digest: Our National Parks, by the Reader's Digest. Pleasantville, NY: The Reader's Digest Association, 1985.

II. Bicycle Touring Books

The Pacific Crest Bicycle Trail, by Bill Paul. Santee, CA: Sunbelt Publications, 1990.

Southwest America Bicycle Route, by Lindsay and Hample. Santee, CA: Sunbelt Publications, 1987.

Cyclists' Route Atlas: A Guide to the Gold Country and High Sierra North, by Randall Gray Braun. Chester, CA: Bodfish Books, 1987.

The Best Bike Rides in New England, by Paul Thomas. Chester, CT: Globe Pequot Press, 1990.

Bicycling the Blue Ridge, by Elizabeth and Charlie Skinner. Birmingham, AL: Menasha Ridge Press.

California Dream Cycling, by Chuck "Bodfish" Elliot. Chester, CA: Bodfish Books, 1990.

Bike Rides of the Colorado Front Range, by Vici De Haan. Boulder, CO: Pruett Publishing, 1981.

Bicycling the Pacific Coast, by Tom Kirkendall and Vicky Spring. Seattle: The Mountaineers Books, 1990.

The American Bicycle Atlas, by Dave Gilbert. New York: E.P. Dutton, 1981.

The Canadian Rockies Bicycling Guide, by Gail Helgason and John Dodd. Edmonton, Alberta, Canada: Cone Pine Publishers.

General Cycling Books

Daisy, Daisy: a journey across America on a bicycle, by Christian Miller. Garden City, NY: Doubleday, 1981.

Miles From Nowhere, by Barbara Savage. Seattle: The Mountaineers Books, 1983.

Bicycle Touring International, by Kameel Nasr. San Francisco: Bicycle Books.

The Complete Guide to Bicycling in Canada, by Elliot Katz. Westminster, MD: Random House.

Bicycle Touring and Camping, by Edward F. Dolan. New York: J. Messner, 1982.

Bike Touring: the Sierra Club guide to outings on wheels, by Raymond Bridge. San Francisco: Sierra Club Books, 1979.

The Traveling Cyclist, by Roy M. Wallack. New York: Doubleday, 1991.

The Bicycle Touring Manual, by Rob van der Plas. San Francisco: Bicycle Books.

Bicycling Book, by John Marino. Boston: Houghton Miffling, 1981.

Greg LeMond's Complete Book of Bicycling, by Greg Lemond, New York, Putnam, 1987.

The Complete Book of Long-Distance and Competitive Cycling, by Tom Doughty. New York: Simon and Schuster, 1983.

INDEX

Index by Paul Kish, Kish Indexing Service, Box 661, Mendocino, CA 95460 (707) 964-2649